# TECH FLUENT CEO

Build and Lead Extraordinary Digital Companies,
Without Being a Tech Nerd

**Aman Y. Agarwal**

## TECH FLUENT CEO

First Edition 2022

Hardcover ISBN: 978-9916-4-1333-3

Paperback ISBN: 978-9916-4-1224-4

E-PUB ISBN: 978-9916-4-1226-8

Published simultaneously in the U.S.A, Canada, United Kingdom, European Union, Australia, India, and Japan.

Distributed globally by Sanpram Transnational Corporation, Ahtri tn 12, Kesklinna Linnaosa, Tallinn City, Estonia - 10151 World Wide Web site address is https://sanpram.com

This is a work of fiction. Names, characters, places, and incidents are either the product of the author's imagination or are used fictitiously, and any resemblance to actual persons, living or dead, business establishments, events, or locales is entirely coincidental.

*To my mother.*

# Table Of Contents

# A Serious Promise

No original book ever written in the history of the world is meant for everyone.

This book is no exception.

So let me make you a promise.

If you read this book and realize you're not the right reader for it, but have already paid for it and the retailer won't take it back, you can email me directly at [aman@sanpram.com] and ask for a full refund.

With that out of the way, let's begin!

Chapter One

# Students of Trade: Movies, Sneakers, and Love Hotels

Although it's customary to give an introduction before diving into the main content, I've chosen to defer things like "why I wrote this book" to the next chapter. First, let's stretch and warm up with a nice little brainstorm about business and innovation.

Imagine it's 1998, and you're starting a business that helps people watch movies at home. One way is to open a physical store where people can buy or rent a VHS tape or a DVD. If you, gentle reader, are too young to know what a VHS tape is, please do not be disheartened — it is for movies what a vinyl record is for music. (Oh wait...)

Most people prefer to rent DVDs than to buy them, and selling is less profitable anyway. You make money every time someone rents a movie at your store. Here's what might go through your mind:

1.  You have to pay for leasing the place and other bills of a physical store. This means high *fixed* costs — which you have to pay every month regardless of whether your business is doing well or poorly. If your monthly bill is $10,000 total then you need to earn that much in revenue to break even.

2.  Let's say every rental costs customers $5. To earn $10,000, you need 2,000 rentals per month — whether you have 2,000 DVDs that get rented only once or 500 DVDs that get rented four times. You just need a minimum *number* of rentals per month to make money. Many DVDs in your inventory will not be popular to rent, and the cost of buying those needs to be recovered from the others. So you'll have to make sure that your *popular* ones circulate a lot: which means customers have to return them *quickly* so that someone else can rent them. Therefore, your business model requires heavily penalizing late returns, or it won't work.

3.  Customers have to visit the store to browse movies. They also carry their DVDs home on their own, so you don't lose any money on the delivery.

4.  Each store can only serve a tiny mile radius of customers, so if you want to scale to the whole country and the world, you need tens of thousands of stores.

A company that had the above model, called Blockbuster, dealt with the same factors. They were the market leader, with 60,000 employees and a *lot* of stores.

On top of that, they held expensive VHS tapes instead of DVDs. A new VHS tape cost them $65 and had to be rented *30 times* before it fully paid for itself! Moreover, most customers wanted to borrow the latest movies and not old ones, and the hot titles usually ran out as soon as they arrived. To force people to return the tapes quickly, they raised late fees so much that it represented 16% of their overall revenue.

Essentially, a customer would walk into a Blockbuster store hoping to watch the newest movie that night, get disappointed that it was already out of stock, have to visit the store several times before *finally* being able to rent it, and then be penalized heavily for not being quick enough to return it.

Unsurprisingly, Blockbuster was slowly failing.

Now, let's ask, what if you wanted to improve the profit margins in such a business, by introducing new technologies and business models? Let's think about it:

1.  If you don't have a physical store, you will save a lot of fixed costs. But then how would you deliver the movie to someone's home? It could be by mailing it in a package, downloading it onto their computer, streaming online, etc. You determine that given the market conditions in 1998 (when most people's internet connection isn't fast enough to play movies without buffering), you'd have to start with mailing DVDs home. Now, if you want to scale to

the whole country, you need very few physical warehouses where you store a lot of DVDs cheaply and use the postal service for deliveries. Theoretically, you can serve every customer in the country from just a single warehouse!

2.  Customers have to mail the DVD back to you, so you pay for postage in both directions. Now, each delivery costs more money than the Blockbuster model (where the customer takes care of delivery). Lower fixed costs, higher *variable* costs — you only pay for postage when you make a sale. A single DVD, once purchased by you, can be rented again by someone halfway across the country, making you money every time. The unit economics seem much better than those of small physical stores.

3.  You've saved some money, but customers still need a way to *browse* the DVDs! Again, there are multiple possible solutions. It's 1998, online shopping is growing quite fast, so you decide that an eCommerce website would be great. It lets the customer browse *way more* movies than in a single store. Another benefit is being able to filter by many more factors — your favorite actor, the date of release, Oscar winners, etc. These are great features that a physical store can't possibly offer. Realize that all these will become *essential* features for your website that give you a significant competitive advantage over stores. By the way, one alternative to online shopping would be to set up a call center helpline where a "concierge" helps you choose a movie over the phone and places the order. Maybe this would be an excellent way to start small and test the whole idea of DVD-by-mail? It's a decision you make carefully.

You decide that many people will prefer your online service to stores, so you put together an engineering team that builds the eCommerce system. You're in business! You start serving some customers better than Blockbuster and make money.

Your business has to deal with *some* of the same problems that Blockbuster does — lost DVDs, late returns, etc. You also still need to charge some late fees, because you are carrying inventory after all. But since you have very low fixed costs, you can be much more lenient.

However, if you look at the whole picture objectively, you still don't have a *huge* competitive advantage.

First, being a small company, people don't know about your little website. They only know Blockbuster and other brands. Second, it takes time for a movie to arrive at someone's home — it doesn't give them the instant pleasure of walking into a store, picking a movie, and watching it the same night. Therefore, you also have to stock up on slightly less popular/niche movies that aren't readily available at most stores — because *your* margins on these movies are much higher than those of Blockbuster! For the same reason, you also consider making your own movies that you can distribute exclusively — but you don't have enough customers to pay for the film production. And third, DVDs are still new, and most people only have a VHS tape player at home, so you have to wait for them to switch before they can become your customers.

To stay competitive, you try to offer a monthly *subscription* service that allows unlimited rentals with no late fees — you just need to return a movie before borrowing another. In the hands of highly active subscribers, this can cost you a fortune (unlimited rentals = unlimited postage at your expense). But it's a very attractive offer, and you spend a lot of money on marketing, so you steadily gain customers, quickly growing your predictable recurring revenue.

This was the story of Netflix. By early 2000, Netflix had become a severely unprofitable two-year-old startup with an unproven business model. They offered to sell the business to Blockbuster for $50 million, believing that its online platform could complement the brick-and-mortar model. Blockbuster refused.

So Netflix decided to keep growing (and keep snatching customers from Blockbuster). They raised money by going public.

After a few years of being in business, Netflix realized that the sands of technology were shifting again — enough people had a fast internet connection such that they could stream movies online. The rise of YouTube, Broadcast.com, and others was also encouraging. Streaming would greatly reduce your costs of delivering a movie to the viewer *immediately*, quicker than both physical stores and eCommerce, while removing the need for physical inventory altogether. Netflix grew so fast that nobody else could catch up.

Phew — that was a lot of brainstorming already, right? The above seems like a clear picture, but I assure you it is not. Marc Randolph, the first CEO of Netflix, came up with the idea of DVD rentals by chance while pitching random ideas to his friend, and not by doing careful analysis like we just did! They had to figure out the rest as they went along.

It's easy to look back in hindsight and chart out a simple David and Goliath story, but there was a lot more going on behind the scenes, with many other players in the market. Building a business is never straightforward – judgments can be clouded by a thousand different things and decisions are never obvious.

Now let's switch gears a little, putting on our technical hat for a second and try to derive some features of an online system for renting DVDs. Since we haven't started with the actual book yet (surprise!), I will keep it at the surface level.

First, you need an interactive website with advanced searching, sorting, and filtering of movies. This is how you compete with the browsing experience in physical stores, so these features are not just "nice to have."

You also want to encourage people to rent again and again (it's the very nature of your business), and one way to do that is to *recommend* movies to customers. This too could be done in many ways. One way is to treat it as an engineering problem:

You'd store the customers' browsing and renting history, collect their feedback on movies, and devise an algorithm to predict which movie people will like. This adds another big set of technical requirements (a suitable *database* for storing this information, etc). In 2006, Netflix offered $1,000,000 to anyone who could beat their recommendation system by 10% – that's how critical it is to their overall business.

Streaming also involves a whole new technology system, as well as the task of negotiating expensive licenses with all the movie studios and distributors — you don't need many permissions to buy and resell DVDs, but you do if you want to play their movies online.

If your customers dislike buffering with a passion, you may want to let them download movies and watch offline through your app. Or, you may choose to reduce or improve the video quality depending on the person's internet speed. As you can imagine, there are plenty of ways you could go, and we will discuss these things in more detail later in the book.

The key takeaway here is that your *business strategy* is the critical foundation on top of which the technical strategy stands. Every single decision you make from a technical standpoint has to be aligned with, or be rooted in the end goals of the business — which usually mean reducing costs, increasing margins, and gaining a *sustained competitive advantage,* as we saw above. There is no value to building technology for its own sake, unless you're running a research lab.

In fact, it's about time we disabuse ourselves of the notion that there exists a "tech industry" with "tech companies." Saying that is redundant, because every company is a tech company (more on this later). Whether you make software, or solar panels, or crunchy cream-stuffed doughnuts, it's just a business at the end of the day. Everything else is a fleeting detail.

Consider that Blockbuster too could have launched a streaming service, but they didn't. They got left behind and went bankrupt. What do you think went wrong with those smart people?

Did they lose because Netflix understood technology more deeply or had better engineers? No, I don't believe technical prowess was to blame. Even if you have the world's best engineers building the most advanced product, it doesn't matter unless it makes sense for the business. (An industry veteran once told me a joke about two business ideas: a food formula that makes cat poop *smell* better, and a food formula that makes cat poop *taste* better. Both are fascinating technical problems requiring scientific brilliance, but I suspect that one of them has a much bigger market than the other.)

Other explanations people propose fall along abstract, almost *woo-woo* concepts like "innovation culture," or the blanket judgment that big companies are "slow to adapt."

Blockbuster is a beloved punching bag for modern business gurus, who say that it was run by slow arrogant idiots. I'm more interested in practical ideas. As far as I'm concerned, an armchair thought leader preaching that big companies "stay nimble" and "innovate" is like a fashion critic telling everyone to look more attractive. You agree with his message, but also want to punch him in the throat.

Blockbuster's CEO at the time, John Antioco, was actually an expert in turning failing companies around. They did see the danger, and they did a lot of things right.

One, they renegotiated the prices of VHS tapes in bulk, so they could always afford to have new releases in stock. Two, they banished the high late fees — costing them $200 million in missed revenue but a smart customer-focused decision for the long-term. Three, they launched *their own* online movie rental service now focused on DVDs, called Total Access, which tried to offer an even better deal than Netflix — you could rent a movie online, return it *at any physical store*, and get a free DVD in exchange immediately.

This combined online-offline package was expensive to get running but got customers excited. Blockbuster's growth began to recover.

Netflix was hit pretty hard. There was a quarter in 2007 when Netflix *lost* 55,000 subscribers. In a funny incident, their CEO Reed Hastings told Wall Street analysts on a call that Blockbuster had thrown "everything but the kitchen sink" at them. The very next day — and this is a true story — he received an actual kitchen sink in the mail from John Antioco.

Netflix's only remaining competitive advantage was their recently launched streaming platform, but it wouldn't save the company if they got crushed financially on the DVD rental side.

However, destiny seemed to have other plans. Blockbuster's shareholders on Wall Street didn't like the cost of their new movies, (especially the lost late fees) and decided to fire the CEO for experimenting with the digital strategy. With Antioco gone, the board severely watered down their digital offerings and *reinstated late fees* — making customers angry again. *Now* the company was really doomed beyond saving, and the rest is history. Regardless of who was at fault, they failed to uphold their promise to customers.

The fundamental key to any resilient, innovative business is to be a "student of your trade."

The reason why businesses get disrupted is that their most important *trading partners* (customers) are able to find a better deal elsewhere. It's as simple as that. What I'm going to say next will sound cynical and harsh. The whole of human history has shown that people are not loyal to anyone, they are only loyal to their own needs and wants. Whether it's our partners in trade or life, they stay with us because we offer the best "deal" at the moment. If they're able to find a better deal elsewhere, it's only a matter of time before they'll switch. This is both a blessing and a curse. As leaders, it's up to us to make sure we're always offering the best deal.

We must always be clear about how we are *engaging in commerce*. Commerce means you do something for somebody, and they do something for you in return — very basic, and as old as humanity itself. Who are your trading partners, and what do they *really* get from your deal? What are you trading? Take any industry, company, product, or service and chip away the bark until you arrive at the pristine, timeless equation of commerce.

Being a student of your trade means relentlessly obsessing over where your value lies, what can be improved, etc. Having this mindset gives you the awareness to notice when reality changes around you (whether it's technology or trends), and take calculated risks.

On a side note, that's also the reason why I dislike using the term "users" for people who use your product or service. Although it has become very prevalent throughout the software industry, not only do I find it a little denigrative, it's also bad for business – its repeated usage in daily conversations makes you forget a lot of useful context and makes you compare apples to oranges. For the simplest example, the "users" of LinkedIn, TikTok, and Twitter behave very differently. By choosing the right term for *your* target customers, whether it's "streamers," "accountants," "fashion shoppers," "pet owners" or "fiction lovers," you can infuse more context into your company's day-to-day conversations and automatically align the whole team around serving *that* persona, not some invisible "user." In this book, we will treat it as a technical term and use it only sparingly.

In the case of Netflix, you could say their trade is *helping people enjoy movies and shows.* Every other thing about their business — the subscription model, choice of technology, etc — is fluid and subject to change. If they had only seen themselves as "helping people rent DVDs," they would never have become a streaming company and been driven out of the market by someone else. Recently, Netflix has been evolving the very format of cinema itself, by introducing "interactive" digital shows such as *Black Mirror: Bandersnatch (2018)* where viewers can actively make decisions for the protagonist like in a video game.

Another company that has taken bold steps is Under Armour — an American fitness and apparel company. They started out making garments that absorb and dry sweat better. By 2013, all their competitors had released their own sweat-wicking offerings, and they couldn't really differentiate themselves in the market. So they took a step back, and broadened their mission from trading sweat-wicking shirts and shoes to *"making athletes better."* They saw a new vision for Under Armour as a digital fitness company.

Through a suite of wearable devices and smartphone applications — all focused on the individual consumer who wants to get more fit and athletic — they would help people track their health, nutrition, sleep and fitness activities, get virtual coaching, and receive suggestions for improvement. The bet was that "data is the new oil" — that owning these applications would give Under Armour the most intimate, actionable data about their customers, helping them sell even more products than before.

After spending a billion dollars on acquisitions and technology development over a period of 7 years, they arguably became the world's leading digital fitness brand with over 250 million everyday athletes. And they still sold more shirts and shoes than ever.

Nintendo is an even more fascinating example — you could say their trade is to *help people play fun games*. Nintendo is not a "video game company." It was founded in 1889 by a Japanese craftsman making playing cards. They did not make their first electronic toy or console until the 1970s. During that time, they once also experimented with running a chain of "love hotels" in Japan (i.e. hotels with rooms and services specially designed for... *active* couples) — although that didn't quite work out for them, you've got to admit you can't argue with the logic.

Nintendo has dominated the gaming world not just once, but multiple times. The *Game Boy*, launched in 1989, enjoyed an 11-year reign in the market but eventually got dethroned by Sony's *PlayStation 2* which launched in 2000. The company then pulled a comeback of sorts, launching the *Nintendo DS* family in 2004 — and *once again* became the best-selling gaming console in the world. The CEO of Nintendo who presided over these moves, the late Satoru Iwata, once famously said: "On my business card, I am a corporate president. In my mind, I am a game developer. But in my heart, I am a gamer."

Be a student of your trade — that's lesson number one from this book.

Now, I can't teach you how to figure out what your trade is and what your customers really want. This is not a strategy or marketing book, and I'm not a business guru.

This is a *technology* book. As we saw earlier, being a "student of our trade" is the critical *lens* through which we will view all technology decisions throughout the book.

Now take a quick break, think about what you've learned so far, and I'll see you in the next chapter!

**Artist: Anne-Sophie Balestrini (France)**

*Scan the (hidden) QR code in this artwork for special bonus content.*

Chapter Two

# Can I Have the Swimming Pool Upside-Down?

A G.M. at Citibank once jokingly told me, "The problem with engineers is that they're eggheads. They know too much."

We shared a good laugh before I told him that I was also an engineer. But all that aside, I did acknowledge a germ of truth in what he said: There's a huge communication gap and *disconnect* between "technical" and "non-technical" people in the industry. I see it every day, even in places like Silicon Valley.

Kevin Plank, the founder of Under Armour, didn't find it easy to get his team's commitment internally when he decided to turbocharge their digital transformation. He lacked a technical background, which further added to his struggle. He once said in an interview: "It wasn't that I didn't know the right answers to be seeking from engineers. I didn't even know the right questions to ask! I'm a sporting goods guy."

And Kevin is a freaking billionaire. He could hire the best engineers. He could line up every top-dollar consulting firm in the world with their seasoned squads of Powerpoint commandos serving him advice all day. Given his network, he could also call on the best technology leaders in the world to chat with. But as the CEO, he found that his *personal* lack of technical fluency was a 100 million dollar bottleneck in itself — not the number of tech wizards he didn't have.

That's because real entrepreneurs only make choices that they understand. It doesn't matter whether they're a fledgling startup founder living off cereal and sleeping on friends' couches, or a billion-dollar CEO — they're fiercely independent thinkers. They can take huge risks and deal with tremendous uncertainty, but they won't follow someone's advice like a lemming unless it makes sense to them.

We all know that CEOs don't get to blame their CFO if they discover that half the management team has been funding their family vacations with embezzled money. In the same vein, they also don't get to blame the CTO or CIO or anybody else if their company's tech strategy falls short.

Gregg Steinhafel, the former CEO of Target, an American retail giant, had to personally resign from the company in 2013 after it suffered a massive data breach from a cyber attack. And Gregg wasn't even a techie. He had been a retail person his entire life, starting from his grandfather's furniture store, and had worked in merchandising at Target for over thirty years. (More on this in Chapter Seven.)

Every modern executive, no matter what their educational background, has been expected to understand things like accounting, finance, operations, and marketing — the traditional "core business skills" that every MBA supposedly has. It used to be that technology was something your I.T. department took care of, or a software product you'd buy.

Today, this is far from true. Companies of all sizes, from small businesses and startups to mega-conglomerates like Disney, have understood that digital tech is a core, strategic aspect of their business, not just a tool they use to automate certain tasks. We're also close to a tipping point where artificial intelligence — not even just "software" as most people know it — will quickly weave itself into the very fabric of every business, in every industry. You have to understand how all this technology works, how to use it as a *strategic business function*, and effectively manage the people who implement it.

Andrew Grove, the former CEO of Intel who transformed them into the world's largest semiconductor company, rightly had this to say: "Only the paranoid survive."

You can complain about the changing, unpredictable times all day long, and the grumpy aunt who lives down the lane will be happy to join you. Or, you can get to work on upgrading your knowledge, skills, and thinking tools for the new digital era. That is, become TECH FLUENT.

By the way, don't get the wrong impression; living in a period of rapid change is FANTASTIC! This is the best time in the history of human civilization to be alive, and with every passing year, we have access to more incredible innovations and opportunities than our ancestors ever had. Of course we have some work to do and things to fix, but I want this book to help you not with a *defensive mindset* (trying to "stay relevant") but rather from an *offensive mindset* (seizing opportunities and being an innovator, not a follower).

If you're reading a book like this, I'm assuming it's because:

- You're an ambitious, highly-motivated person who is transitioning towards leading a tech company as a founder, CEO, or executive.

- You don't consider yourself a software engineer or techie, and have no interest in becoming one. You've spent your whole life learning and doing other things.

- You want to use your current knowledge, background, and history of experiences as a powerful asset, not something that holds you back from leading or thriving in a digital future.

- You have an insatiable desire to learn new things and figure out how to solve any problems in your way. You don't want to stagnate; you want to grow more, do more and be more than you already are.

If that describes you, then I admire your spirit, and you're reading the right book.

## The journey to technical fluency

In recent times, the label of being non-technical has almost become a badge of shame that signifies some sort of deficiency. It gives many professionals an innate insecurity, or some variant of impostor syndrome, that they're becoming increasingly irrelevant and are second-class citizens of the industry when compared to engineers. They don't trust what they already know, thinking they could be wrong or sound stupid, and they don't know what they *should* know, thus unable to ask good questions.

Non-technical professionals are constantly told that the path to being tech-fluent is to "learn to code," or some other kind of intense education. That's *terrible* advice. It's useful for people trying to switch careers, but not if your goals are different.

Okay, it's good to give it a try, and if you enjoy it, great — I'm cheering for you. It's just that nobody tells you that this "become a pseudo-engineer" route does surprisingly little to improve your technical fluency unless you spend 12-18 months on dedicated daily practice.

The "learn to code" advice is popular to pass around simply because it's an easy task to *teach* people how to code. Teaching people to develop technical intuition and systems-thinking is much harder, so nobody does it.

And that's exactly why I wrote this book.

This is the book I wish I had when I first started out. It will take you on a fun journey of adventure into the world of digital technologies and software engineering, through interesting case studies from many industries. I'll meet you at your current technical level, and take you much further. Whether you're a non-techie with zero interest in coding, or you've taken months of programming classes, this book will be your friend.

My goal is to help you build up the knowledge and capacity to have an engaged discussion with highly experienced engineers, ask intelligent questions, and be a valuable influence on important tech decisions (whether they go your way or not is less important).

This book contains the same core program that I've personally taught to many entrepreneurs, executives, and professionals belonging to diverse industries from gold mining to banking, and spread all over the globe — now made a thousand times more affordable and accessible.

**What to expect**

This book is roughly divided into three phases, but they're highly interconnected and build on top of each other.

First, we'll start with the intuitive fundamentals of software systems, getting a broad overview of all the different aspects: how computers work, programming languages and frameworks, APIs, etc. We'll also learn how to drive engineering projects to success, learning lessons from billion-dollar disasters at organizations like the FBI and NASA, and becoming aware of critical semi-technical factors like development strategy and engineering culture.

In the next phase, we will dive into the inner workings of complex applications and systems. You'll get a re-introduction to the internet, revealing the layers and protocols that hold the digital world together. We'll discuss the story of modern databases, and see what old libraries can teach us about information management. After that, we will take it up a notch and talk about scalability – seeing how systems and applications scale to millions and billions of users, etc, including case studies ranging from beverage companies to dating websites. We'll wrap up the technical deep dive with cybersecurity, which is now a mainstream concern for every business leader, and learn from the creativity and sophistication of bank robbers.

In the third phase, we will put all the technical knowledge to use, and learn how to actually go about designing software systems that create the efficiency gains and competitive advantages that we're looking for. We'll also take a brief look inside the day-to-day operations of a software engineering organization – things like version control, DevOps, testing and deployment strategy, and so on. And finally, we'll explore the game-changing potential of artificial intelligence, where it's going, and some best practices for how to implement it the right way.

It's worth keeping in mind that technologies constantly change and evolve, so our focus will always be on concepts, not memorizing facts. You can keep this book by your side for many years and it will still be relevant.

The toughest, most perplexing decisions that we face are those that we have no frameworks for. Often, the hardest thing isn't the decision itself, but rather *how to think about* the decision and figure out which questions you should be asking yourself. Without a process to lean on, the analytical devils inside our minds can run wild towards different priorities and paralyze us.

Therefore, the #1 thing I want you to take away from this book is not the knowledge (though it's also important), but rather the frameworks and intuition. It's one of the reasons I like Ray Dalio's book *Principles*. You should read it.

This is probably a good time to introduce myself. My name is Aman, and as an engineer I've worked on self-driving trucks, brain-computer interfaces, robot assistants, and other things. I also worked in B2B sales and partnerships for two large tech startups in Silicon Valley, both worth >$1 billion. I started my career doing a variety of odd gigs, like fixing Coca Cola spills on Macbook keyboards and selling roses on the street (surprisingly lucrative).  In my spare time, I host two podcasts that I love: The Age of AI, and The Eccentric CEO.

As a writer and educator, my passion lies in making hard things simple. I believe that when things are simple, everyone benefits. Simplicity is underrated. I've been lucky to have received worldwide recognition for my teaching, such as being a guest lecturer on AI and creativity for fine arts students in Japan, and my essays on cutting-edge AI being widely discussed and translated by the media in multiple languages. We also work with grassroots organizations and local governments in Africa to develop technical fluency among youth at a larger scale.

On a personal note, I'm a lifelong learner of foreign languages, an avid Judo practitioner, overly sophisticated smoothie chef, and apex predator to all things tofu.

## The best leaders look under the hood

Now I'll take a few examples, but hear a quick disclaimer first. I originally didn't want to use the example of Steve Jobs in this book, because it's very cliché and any discussion of people like him tends to descend into idol worship. I'll still use his example and a few others, but only for a habit that's *extremely common* among successful entrepreneurs. (And it's not the only habit that makes them great.) You can always learn from successful people, but you don't have to be *exactly* like anyone else to succeed.

Wozniak said this about Jobs in his biography: *"Steve didn't ever code. He wasn't an engineer and he didn't do any original design, but he was technical enough to alter and change and add to other designs."*

Jobs was known to have his hand in everything at Apple — be it design, marketing, engineering, or even their factory floor plans which he adopted from Sony, his favorite company in the world. He'd probe deep into critical technical decisions the engineers were making, asking question after question until he was satisfied that their approach made sense in light of the company goals.

Even though Jobs wasn't an engineer himself, he was known for incredible intuition that often drove engineers to the very limits of their knowledge with his inquisitiveness. Many times he would anticipate technical challenges as well as potential solutions *before* an engineer even finished explaining, and leap ahead in the discussion to cut to the root of the issue.

Consider some basic questions that might often arise at a business like Apple's:

- What tech do you patent, what do you keep as a trade secret, and what do you open-source?

- When do you use someone else's technology and when do you develop your own?

- What type of R&D do you invest in?

- What external platforms do you support officially and unofficially? For example, would you allow other smartphones companies to install iOS on their phones? Should you put USB ports on the Macbook? Do you just use Bluetooth or create your own proprietary wireless system exclusive to Apple devices?

All these decisions are complex and fairly technical and must be made as a team, but it can be essential for the CEO to have a say on them. Your own business may not be that tech-heavy, but there are always things that come up that would be relevant to you.

Bill Gates had an even more intense reputation at Microsoft — he went so far as to personally check *every line of code* of the software for the first several years. Elon Musk has an obsession with the details at all his companies — he talks in-depth with all engineering teams, whether it's about esoteric manufacturing processes, semiconductor chips, or rocket propulsion. Jeff Bezos famously made an *executive* mandate back in 2002 as the CEO of Amazon, about how all engineering teams must stick to only API-based service architectures or they'd be fired (more about this in later chapters).

For some non-tech examples, Nike founder Phil Knight personally made trips to shoe factories all over the world for decades, being closely involved in their setup and logistics end-to-end, because some of those details can have huge consequences on the business. Manufacturing and logistics weren't even remotely his specialty or "background" — he was just a running enthusiast at heart who hated Adidas. For a long time after starting Nike, he still worked as a part-time accounting professor. (By the way, his autobiography *Shoe Dog* is one of my most beloved books of all time.)

Aliko Dangote, the Nigerian industrialist and wealthiest man in all of Africa as of 2022 (you should know his name if you don't already), was once asked by the American billionaire David Rubenstein for his top business advice. He simply said, "You have to know your business A to Z." He said he personally does in-depth study into every single business his conglomerate gets into — whether it's the chemical composition of the fertilizers they produce, or the technical specifications of his petroleum refineries, cement factories, and power plants. Mukesh Ambani, India's wealthiest industrialist, has the same quality.

I could go on and on, but basically, it doesn't matter what your background is. If something is critical to your business, you should understand it and have an independent opinion on it.

## You don't need permission

In too many tech companies, for non-technical managers, "collaboration with engineers" really means that engineers declare to them in jargon-laden terms how things should be, while they politely nod, give up on trying to understand what's going on, and then wonder to themselves afterward: "Well we *were* in a meeting, so I guess we collaborated by default?"

No, that's called living in denial. That meeting was not only a waste of everyone's time, but it probably had a negative effect — because now everyone is under the false illusion that they've "communicated" and are on the same page when they may not be. It will likely cost extra time, money, and sobbing in the bathroom later on.

I know it's hard to ask probing questions to senior engineers, let alone push back on them, especially when it was so difficult to hire them in the first place (as we know, they don't come cheap or easy).

And to be fair, there's also a flip side — often engineers are driven crazy with absurd timelines and demands made by decision-makers who have no idea what they're really asking for. Imagine hiring an architect to build your new house (congrats) and having this conversation:

- "I've always wanted a swimming pool in my kitchen. Can we have it upside-down?"

- "Yes, if we launch your house into space and place it properly in orbit."

- "Great! Since this is just a small change, we won't have any extra budget for this and still need to stick to the 5-month deadline."

- "Wait, that's not what I meant..."

As a leader, whenever you decide to not get too involved in a technical discussion, I want to empower you to be the one to choose so, intelligently — to do it because you clearly understand the context of the discussion and can see exactly why you don't need to be involved. Don't relegate oversight just because you feel handicapped by your knowledge and at the mercy of whatever someone tells you.

To be clear, this book is NOT about coming across as a control freak or showing people who's boss. You won't micromanage them and negotiate over every decision they make — that's a recipe for disaster. That would make any good engineer quit within a week. (At least I would.) If you do this as a CEO, this type of behavior could further facilitate the creation of "factions" within your company, with the techies seeing the CTO as their real leader, "protecting them" from you and the others.

In my experience, the very best engineers greatly *appreciate* when non-techies and beginners take an interest in their work and are willing to learn. A true professional will never make you feel "stupid" when you ask them a genuine question — on the contrary, they'll make a sincere effort to support and educate you.

Some engineers could see your well-intended involvement as a waste of their time, or at worst, a threat to themselves. They'll want you to do "your thing" (fundraising, marketing, sales, hiring, etc.) and let them do "their thing." 99% of the time it's not personal. They just don't trust your ability to understand what they're doing. Once they see that even if you're a tenderfoot in technology, you're not a total ignoramus, you will develop mutual respect within a remarkably short time. (And I hope we've already established that there's no "your thing" and "their thing." If everything's going to be your fault in the end, it automatically becomes your thing.)

Now, I have to admit — there *are* a few bad apples in our industry, who subconsciously believe and act as if anyone who's not an engineer automatically has a lower IQ, but those are a small minority. At the end of the day, you can't please everybody all the time and accommodate everyone's ego, so you just have to be unapologetic about it.

Good technical communication is a two-way street. While you make sincere efforts to improve your technical fluency, it's also *their job* to explain their work to you and bridge the gap from their end.

This is why, besides the knowledge building, throughout this book we'll also touch frequently on the theme of how to gain healthy influence over engineers — how to be seen as a value-add and not a nuisance, and how to know *where* to draw the line in terms of your involvement.

Let me also give you some "realistic" or "cynical" reassurance if you need any. It's tempting to believe that every single engineer around you is an A+ player and knows what they're doing, and has considered every alternative so you have nothing to offer. But the data doesn't agree.

The harsh reality is that *most* tech projects fail — by completely missing deadlines, going out of scope, running out of budget, and even products being discarded altogether *after* being finished because they weren't necessary in the first place. Talk to any senior executive in any industry (especially banking and finance folks) — they'll tell you how they've been burned before, and have learned the hard way that you can't just let the technical folks freely do whatever they see fit.

It's essential to be empathetic and open and listen to experts, and let the pros do their jobs. I want you to engage and guide them towards ideas that *you* find important.

## "Don't trust the experts"

In October 2017, I was at a small private gathering of self-driving car engineers in Mountain View, California. Among us was Sebastian Thrun, who is considered the godfather of modern autonomous vehicles.

Sebastian told us a most intriguing story about how his journey began. In 2005, his team at Stanford had won the DARPA Grand Challenge, which was to build a completely self-driving car that raced across *other* self-driving cars in a desert. By 2009, he was renowned as the worldwide expert on autonomous robots, unquestionably at the very top of the field.

Then he got a call from Larry Page, who had an unusual proposal.

He asked Thrun if he'd like to come over to Google and build autonomous cars that could drive on *every street in California*, whether downtown San Francisco or the interstate highways.

Thrun flat out said no. "It's impossible, can't be done." They had gone crazy building a car that could finish a race in the middle of a *desert* or at most in an empty town at 10-15mph, and here Page was asking to drive it through crowded streets and traffic lights, with sneaky little monsters (also called "children" by some people) running around. The complexity of the challenge would explode.

But Page wouldn't give in easily. The abrupt verdict didn't make sense to him.

He came back the next day. He acknowledged that Thrun was the expert and that he'd trust his opinion that it was impossible. But he added a clever legitimate question: "Can you give me a *technical reason*, just so I can explain it to Sergey [Brin] why it just can't be done?"

"And I thought and thought and thought for the whole day, but I couldn't come up with a technical reason. It had just been my gut feeling based on how hard it was," Thrun said.

So Page said, if there's even a 10% chance that Thrun was wrong, it was worth a try! Maybe they'd save millions of lives who die in road accidents every year. Thrun admitted defeat and joined Google soon after.

This is the story of how Sebastian Thrun became the founder of Google X. The self-driving car project was the first step in Page's dream of a semi-secret research lab that tackles "moonshot challenges" that could change the course of civilization. Google X is now a separate company under Alphabet, simply called X.

Within 18 months, Thrun's team was successful in building a car that logged 1,000 consecutive miles, *without* human intervention, on most streets in California.

Thrun shared that he now felt embarrassed about this experience. It taught him a humbling lesson about the difference between an *expert* and a *visionary*. "Don't trust the experts," he said. "I was *the* world expert, and I was wrong. Experts tend to know the past, but nobody's an expert on the future."

Some people might hate me for admitting this publicly: you can unleash incredibly valuable insights from your non-technical background and experience that engineers probably don't have.

Engineering at the highest level is about creative problem-solving, using the knowledge and tools at your disposal. Engineering is very subjective. It's not like one of those math exams you had in school where there was only one right answer and one right formula. If it was, there would be no concept of "design" — every product on your desk, every vehicle, every building would look the same, and there would be barely any innovation. Design and creativity are inseparable from engineering.

Repeat after me: *"Engineering is a CREATIVE profession."*

Creative ideas are no one's monopoly. The most creative solutions and inspiration come from outside a domain of expertise, not from inside it.

You use WiFi, GPS, and Bluetooth, right? Say thanks to Hedy Lamarr — co-inventor of the *frequency-hopping spread spectrum* that made these technologies possible. She was also one of the most celebrated Hollywood actresses of the 20th century. You should read about her sometime.

Let me make another bold claim while we're at it. I believe that the Age of AI is really the golden age of creatives, liberal arts, and natural sciences. While there's more demand for technical talent than ever before, in reality, a lot of the menial parts of engineering are quickly getting automated or abstracted away. The more rudimentary programming jobs — which are getting outsourced to "cheaper" geographies anyway — will slowly disappear altogether, being performed by AI. And trust me, the very best engineers *know this*. They have no interest in winning the "programming olympics"; they understand that they're paid to find innovative solutions to problems instead.

As much as it hurts me to say this, the industry doesn't need more "keyboard monkeys," but rather well-rounded problem solvers who can offer diverse perspectives using both technical *and* non-technical knowledge. In other words, it needs what I'd call *Renaissance Entrepreneurs.*

## A final word before we start

I don't finish most books that I begin reading. And I totally empathize if you're the same way.

You don't have to finish this book to get good value from it, and you don't even have to revise the material again and again.

I've intentionally written the book for impatient people like myself, such that once you finish a chapter, you can start putting your newfound knowledge to use immediately. As you go from one topic to another, you'll also keep reinforcing concepts, so I simply won't let you forget what you learned.

Therefore, as the author I give you my full, wholehearted permission to *stop reading at any point,* never return to the book again, and not feel guilty. No pressure.

But in the same vein, I will also guarantee that you WILL get exponentially more value the further you read, so I do recommend that you finish the book!

I also recommend getting a physical copy to get the most out of this book. Put your phone on silent, turn off the computer, grab a pen, highlight things, and scribble notes. Go back to your school days.

As your "teacher" and guide on this journey, I'll strive to earn your attention every step of the way and make it worth your while. Let's go.

**Artist: M. Lutfi' As'ad, S.Si. (Indonesia)**

*Scan this artwork like a QR code for optional bonus content.*

Chapter Three

# The Ultimate Cooking Guide to Software

Time to officially begin your technical fluency journey! This chapter is a fun, breezy introduction to the modern world of software technologies. You'll build a solid foundation and get a "big picture" overview that motivates you to go deeper into the advanced topics that come later.

We will cover a lot of ground, and your humble teacher is not known for his taciturnity, so take it slow and chill for the next 30-40 minutes. I'll prompt you to take breaks periodically.

**We're going to cook a meal.**

Foma and Lusha are having dinner tonight. You are the chef responsible for making it happen.

The following high-level things are required for this dinner:

1.  Ingredients

2.  Someone to cook the meal

3.  Space (for storing food and for cooking)

4.  A recipe

5.  Tools and equipment (and maybe fuel) for cooking and serving, etc.

As you can see from the attention to detail in the chef's beard, I'm a gifted artist and calligrapher.

None of these things alone would be sufficient, and each one is critical. Here's the kicker: Every computer system is a kitchen, and all software/computing is essentially a way to achieve these five things and tailor them to different kinds of "meals."

We *need* to start with the basic building blocks of a computer. This high-level cooking analogy will serve you well for almost every software system you imagine in the future.

In a computing system, you have information and inputs (or **data**) that act as ingredients, and based on that data, you have to generate a result that can be consumed by someone else, like a meal.

Every computer has a **processor**, or a processing unit (CPU), that acts as the cook (or team of cooks). This processor works with the ingredients (data) and is part of the physical hardware.

The cook also needs space. First, this is where you can *store* things permanently, like the fridge, etc. In your personal computer, this is referred to as ***disk space***—the free space in your hard drive where you store all your files.

Then, there needs to be counter space for cooking. It's extremely hard to cook a meal if you only have your fridge and a stovetop, and no space to work on! In computing, this "working space" is referred to as ***memory*** or *RAM* (random access memory). RAM is not occupied by an item permanently – it can be used for different meals as the need arises, but usually, it's a limited amount of space.

As you can expect, if you run out of working space on the counters due to too many cooks and stuff in the kitchen, it is harder to extend than storage space! The same is true for RAM – my current computer has 8 GB of memory but over 120 GB of storage.

Over the years as technology has developed, processors have become faster, and both the storage space and working memory of computers have greatly expanded.

In the 80s, 10 MB of disk space cost >$3,000. Today, you can buy 100,000 times this space for $50.

By the way, ingredients can come from the storage, and they can also be new ingredients coming fresh from outside that only sit on the counter/table, go straight into the meal, and never make it into storage. Say Foma brings fresh basil and requests the chef to add it to the dish.

There can also be other kinds of inputs to the kitchen, such as pieces of *information* that act as commands, e.g., Lusha telling you that she is allergic to basil.

Or even the order itself, e.g., "Poutine for my dog please." (Just kidding, Canadians I love you). From a software point of view, all these inputs are just different kinds of data (i.e., ingredients).

Then, there needs to be a recipe for the dish that the processor/cook must execute with the data. This recipe is called *software* (or "code", "software program," "program" etc). We will talk about software/recipes in more detail later.

Finally, various tools and equipment are needed for different ingredients and recipes. A kitchen also has some rules and protocols for how things work, which is especially true for professionally run kitchens. This collection of tools and kitchen rules makes up the *operating system* of a computer, and these things have an impact on what kind of recipes can be executed in a given kitchen.

For example, a "kitchen" designed only for brewing beer may not be able to handle an order for spicy barbecued pineapple pizza. (I'm sorry if you don't like pineapple pizza because you were not gifted with an elevated sense of taste.) Operating systems come in families of varieties like Macintosh, Windows, Linux, etc. – each is unique in some way.

As a recap, your computer has a **processor** that does all the work; it has space of two types: **disk storage** and **RAM/memory**; it has **software programs** that act as recipes executed on **data**. Depending on the specific **operating system** of the computer, recipes/software are executed differently. I'll keep using these terms interchangeably until we trick your mind into remembering the concepts forever!

This is a good time to take a 2-minute break and reflect on what you just learned.

# Software technology is very much like a food business.

Let's talk more about recipes/software programs. I want you to read this particular section more slowly because it will get dense soon.

In the modern world, a recipe is usually "high-level" and includes smaller sub-recipes and functions. This is called the level of abstraction.

Say a recipe for Thai Curry requires tofu as an ingredient. Now, tofu is a recipe in its own right – you have to grow soybeans, boil them, and make the bean curd in a hundred different ways. If you have a *high-level recipe*, it *doesn't care how you get tofu*. It treats tofu as a finished **object.**

It may also use verbs like "sauté," "simmer," and "chop," and assume you know what they mean. These are called *functions*. For someone who has never cooked before, these are probably too high-level. They'll have to look up how to sauté and how to simmer.

A recipe can be written in **high-level** or **low-level** language. In a high-level language, you assume the cook can interpret the meaning of "sauté" and "simmer" and also procure "tofu" on their own. In a low-level language, the recipe would ditch the abstractions and instead explain things in very lengthy detail, like how exactly to make tofu, how to sauté, etc.

Just like it's easier to express certain things in French or Japanese compared to English, in the software world, we have many programming languages with unique characteristics. But ultimately they all just tell a computer's processor how to work with data and produce the desired "meal". Some engineers prefer a certain kind of language to another, depending on the task or how they've been trained.

A chef trained at *Le Cordon Bleu* would understand French cuisine and its lingo/jargon (with their "mother sauces" and everything), while a chef trained at a Japanese hibachi or yakitori restaurant may prefer her recipes in a different style.

So you also have different programming languages like Python, JavaScript, and Ruby. These are considered high-level, so they're simpler to read and write, and pack a lot of common features and objects as abstractions without going into detail. Python, in particular, is so high-level that the code looks almost like speaking plain English. The vast majority of programmers today write code in high-level languages.

```
Word = "Hello"

Letters = [ ]

for w in Word:
    print(w)
    if w == "e":
        print("What a funny letter")
```

No need to understand this, but this is what high-level code looks like (this language is Python).

Then you also have low-level programming languages – these are very explicit and describe the program in great detail with fine-tuned control. Naturally, these programs are much longer than those written in high-level languages but also tend to be more efficient – they are used for high-performance computing. They need the programmer to have a certain level of mastery.

After all, if you're writing a recipe and use a low-level language with careful, precise control of the temperature at each step and the exact ratio of salt to turmeric, *you better know what you're doing*. For most dishes, it won't change the final product much. The same is true for programming.

Usually, a programmer is proficient in only a select few programming languages, but depending on the company/project she works in, she sometimes has to learn a new language to some degree to collaborate with her teammates. Just like you would have to if you moved to a different country.

```
VRTSTART    TS  WCHVERT
# Page 601
        CAF TWO     # WCHPHASE = 2 ---> VERTICAL : P65,P66,P67
        TS  WCHPHOLD
        TS  WCHPHASE
        TC  BANKCALL    # TEMPORARY, I HOPE HOPE HOPE
        CADR    STOPRATE    # TEMPORARY, I HOPE HOPE HOPE
        TC  DOWNFLAG    # PERMIT X-AXIS OVERRIDE
        ADRES   XOVINFLG
        TC  DOWNFLAG
        ADRES   REDFLAG
        TCF VERTGUID


033911,000064: 32,3017    06037    FLAGORGY    TC    INTPRET    # DIONYSIAN FLAG WAVING

034090,000243: 32,3241    13247    02F    P63SPOT4    # BRANCH IF ANTENNA ALREADY IN POSITION 1
034091,000244:
034092,000245: 32,3242    33254    CAF    CODE500    # ASTRONAUT:    PLEASE CRANK THE
034093,000246: 32,3243    04616    TC    BANKCALL    #    SILLY THING AROUND
034094,000247: 32,3244    20623    CADR    GOPERF1
034095,000248: 32,3245    16001    TCF    GOTOP00H    # TERMINATE
034096,000249: 32,3246    13235    TCF    P63SPOT3    # PROCEED    SEE IF HE'S LYING

034101,000254: 32,3251    04635    TC    POSTJUMP    # OFF TO SEE THE WIZARD ...
034102,000255: 32,3252    74126    CADR    BURNBABY
```

This is what low-level code looks like. I can't even begin to read it myself. Fun fact: it is believed that both these fragments of code were written for the Apollo 11 mission! Read the funny code "comments" that the programmers left on the right side, separated from the main code with a # sign.

Fun fact: low-level programmers often get paid a lot, and (I might get crucified for saying this) *tend to be older*. But since I've said it now, here goes another:

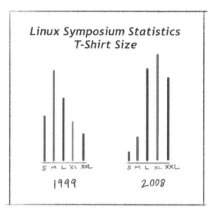

Linux Symposium 2008

A computer's machinery only understands the lowest of the low-level languages. All high-level code is automatically translated by the operating system into low-level code by a little thing called a *compiler* (which is itself a little piece of software whose only job is translation), so that the programmer (the recipe writer) doesn't have to explain too much. Isn't that beautiful? I think computers are so beautiful.

On the other extreme, you've probably heard of **No-Code** tools that let you create software without writing *any* code – they now range from simple drag 'n' drop website builders to some pretty sophisticated products. You could say they're an even *higher* level of a programming language than Python or JavaScript. It is called "no-code," but I still consider it programming – it's just that instead of *only* using your keyboard and a text editor, you're using the mouse or trackpad and have a more visual user interface.

## Programming Frameworks

Even when using the same language, you can write a recipe in many different ways in terms of how you order and organize the information and instructions visually on paper. This adds some style to the recipes. For example, it's fairly common to list the ingredients first, separate from the instructions.

Imagine if the whole recipe was a list of instructions one by one, with ingredients introduced in-between. The final dish would be exactly the same since the actual recipe doesn't change, but for some people, a recipe *written* this way could become much more difficult to follow and make changes to. (See figure.)

Some recipes also introduce their own internal objects and functions, to help you write higher-level code in the same language. For example, say you had a cookbook that uses *soft-boiled eggs* or *poached egg*s as recurring ingredients in multiple dishes. For those who don't know how to soft-boil or poach eggs, the cookbook could include a chapter or appendix that covered different egg boiling techniques once and then freely used those terms repeatedly throughout. The cookbook's author basically uses *their own framework* for writing recipes.

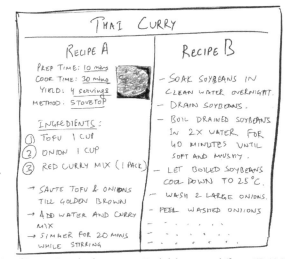

Recipe A and Recipe B are both written in English but using different FRAMEWORKS. Each makes use of different in-built objects and functions.

Since software engineers work on reeeeaaalllly large recipes, it makes sense to devise and follow some common sense principles and best practices for organizing their code to make it readable, reusable, maintainable, and easily modifiable.

Using a framework greatly accelerates the development of most kinds of software applications. They also often give you a lot of reusable code blocks to handle common things – for example, handling user logins and password security etc., in a web application. The fewer the custom/unusual features and functionalities of a software application and the more mature (tried and tested) the frameworks are, the quicker it can be built.

Due to the power of frameworks and reusable code, the *basic* functionality of a website like the New York Times, which is just a fancy blog from a technical standpoint, can be built in as little as a week or two. Any extra time would go into special features that have to be written from scratch. Because of this, much of current software development is like "Lego Engineering." It's much more about using templates and blocks that already exist than what the previous generation of programmers had to deal with, as they often built their own tools from scratch. (More on this in later chapters.)

If you ever have an app idea that you hire a team of freelance engineers to build, being able to estimate how many features are fairly standard and which ones are more custom/unique to your application will help you not get scammed into overpaying for very simple stuff. Although reading this chapter alone won't prepare you for such situations right away, I want to plant that seed in your head.

Now, since a framework essentially represents an *opinion* about how code should be organized and written, naturally there is a lot of disagreement, so there are multiple frameworks available for different languages. At this point I don't need you to memorize any names, but I'll mention a few.

For Python-based web applications, two popular frameworks are Flask and Django. But to use Python for "deep learning" (a sub-field within machine-learning we'll discuss in Chapter Ten), two such frameworks are TensorFlow and PyTorch. For JavaScript applications, well, let's just leave that alone for now because there's a whole framework circus going on for that poor language.

For every programming language, there are different frameworks available for different kinds of applications, and all of them help make a programmer's job easier. Just like public opinion, many frameworks are like trends. They come and go.

**Quick Summary:**

- Programming (recipe writing) is a way to communicate instructions to the processor (cook).

- There are different languages and different ways to program the exact same instructions.

- Code can be high-level, using functions and objects already defined by other people for common tasks. It can also be low-level. The lower the level, the more fine-tuned control you get over the computer.

- All high-level code automatically gets translated into low-level code by a compiler.

- Even for the same language, there are various opinions and best practices about how to write a recipe so that it's easily readable, reusable, maintainable, editable, etc. These opinions and practices are packaged as "frameworks."

Okay, this is a very good time to take a short break and review what you just learned.

Did you know that baby penguins sneeze louder than most dogs can bark? Actually, this is not true but I decided to put something funny here to force you to take a break.

# The Modern Internet Company

Now that you have at least a fuzzy intuition about software, I want to do an overview of the modern tech "stack." Let's learn about servers, back-ends, front-ends, and databases.

Before the internet became popular, if you wanted to benefit from using a software application, you had to buy it on a CD or floppy drive and run it entirely on your computer. This means you would have to use your computer's resources (processors, memory, and storage) to do *everything*. In culinary terms, if you lived on the other side of a big town, you couldn't get food delivered to your home from a restaurant – you had to buy their recipe and cook it in your own kitchen all by yourself because delivering it fresh and hot would be impossible.

But what if there was a dedicated motor highway allowing food to be transported to your customer's home in less than 10 minutes? Wow. Now, if your customers just want a good meal with your recipe at their home, they don't have to cook the thing themselves. The average home kitchen is not sophisticated enough to properly cook your fancy recipes anyway. You can prepare the dish and deliver it to them fresh and hot. Now the preparation of the food *(the back-end)* and the plating & eating *(the front-end)* can be separated by great distances.

Enter the internet! Now that computers can directly connect with each other and share data at great speeds, any heavy computation can occur on one computer, and it can send only the results of that computation to another computer! Now, just one person (say Google) can invest in massive and powerful computers that crunch millions of web pages every second, and you with your little laptop can benefit from their computation power by getting the search results you want, served on a platter through your web browser.

In this system, Google acts as the **back-end** of the search application, and the page you see when you open google.com is just the **front-end.** On the back-end, they have massive sophisticated 'kitchens' – trillions of processors, billions of bytes of storage space and memory and whatnot, and your PC (or even phone!) can access the fruits of their labor.

The faster the internet gets, the **more** things can be done over the internet in *remote* kitchens. As you can see here, internet speed is a constraint that engineers always have to play with while designing their systems.

Today you can "stream" more and more data from the internet than ever before. Remember Netflix? While 15–20 years ago it was not fun to play movies online due to long buffering times, today's laptops don't even need a slot for DVDs. It's a testament to how many things can now be delegated to the "back-end."

By the way, 5G internet is already here. That's like having warp-speed connections between devices compared to previous generations, so the systems around us will likely become even more fragmented and distributed.

### Clients and Servers

Modern devices are quite varied – laptop computers, smartwatches, mobile phones, tablets, etc. So a good web service (say Facebook) has to accommodate all these different possible **clients** on the front-end and make sure it's easy to use for everyone. Nowadays, client devices are getting even more unique – smart toasters, refrigerators, and even automatic pet feeders that connect to the internet!

The semi-buzzword some people use to describe all *web-based* software is **cloud.** "Cloud-based applications", "cloud computing" and whatnot – it's just someone else's computer. It simply means that much of the heavy computation doesn't happen on your own computer.

The computers on the back-end are called **servers.** They basically run copies of the same software application, one for each client. These servers often share one huge common storage space but have a lot of individual RAM (or working memory). The more copies of your software you can create, the more users your product can support at the same time. This is called **scaling** – just think about how you would 'scale' a food business to serve more and more customers. Companies invest a lot of effort and money to make sure their product/service can scale. We'll discuss this in more detail in Chapter Six.

Now, the common storage space for data on the back-end is extremely well organized so that servers can retrieve and deposit data to it as efficiently as possible. It's called the **database.** There are different kinds of databases that organize and store data differently.

This is not trivial. The development of these modern software databases truly changed the world in an unthinkable manner. Before they came along, everything was done through digital files or even *on paper*. If you wanted to withdraw money from your bank in Berlin, and then fly to Tokyo and do the same, you couldn't – they'd have to make phone calls or telegrams or emails to make sure everyone has the same information about your bank balance. Databases allow you to easily have the *consistency* of information across distances. (More on this in Chapter Five.)

Buying something online, reading Wikipedia, social networking, using an ATM— you're always interacting with a database. **Databases are the backbone of our modern digital world.**

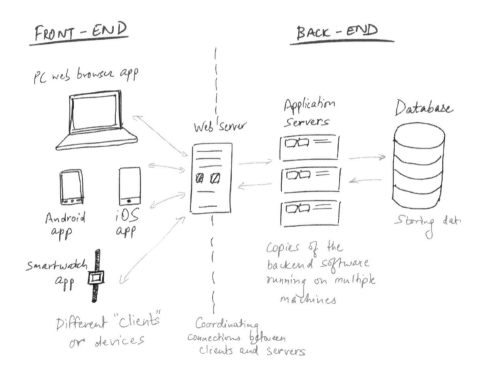

Each individual component of this distributed system performs a unique function and has different software/code running on it.

If you work closely with engineers, you may hear the word **stack**. Although the word itself has several meanings, in this context it is just a description of the particular brand or flavor of each of the things that make up the back-end and front-end. Just like you describe your kitchen to a friend. Engineers love having conversations and debates about stacks. It's like a nerdy discussion about your favourite kitchen appliances and grocery brands – some can even get cultish about it.

To take a quick example, a website I built a while back (DenseLayers) had the following stack:

- Back-end server: *Python* (language), *Flask* (framework)

- Front-end: *HTML5, CSS3* and *JavaScript* (languages), *jQuery* (a library/ framework for *JavaScript*)

- Database: *Postgres*

- Computing (processing power): I'd need powerful computers to scale to millions of users, but don't want to own such computers. So I rent them from a company which also manages them for me. These rented servers use the Linux operating system.

DenseLayers only worked on web browsers. If I also wanted to build mobile apps, I would have to expand the stack further. Consider too that the more things you add to your stack and the more unique it is, the more engineers (and salaries) you need to put into the project.

Moreover, this probably wouldn't be apparent to you, but the stack I use is very simple, fitting the simplicity of my website. If I was building something that needed the sophistication and performance requirements of Google or YouTube, I'd have to use more esoteric languages and frameworks, and also hire other people who know them well.


**Quick Summary:**

It's possible, and sometimes necessary to separate the different functions of a software system and create a complex network. Due to the speed of modern communication technology, these separations could span huge distances – giving birth to the internet. The internet is essentially a complex network of people cooking, storing, serving, and eating each other's food. It feels like the internet is a "thing", but it's just like a large intertwined economy.

# The Global Economy of Software

Let me introduce a concept called APIs. In line with what we discussed earlier, in the modern world, we often sit on the shoulders of giants. Other people already provide services and products that you don't have to create yourself.

We access these services through "Application Programming Interfaces" (APIs). (That's a mouthful right there.) An API is a collection of *rules and protocols* for how to interface with a service. Here's an example:

A lady who sells fish has a different way of doing business than a man who sells newspapers.

A fisherwoman needs you to tell her the type of fish you want, the volume/weight, and maybe some other things. If you can't tell her any of this information, it will be awkward to stand there, and she won't be able to sell you fish.

A newspaper salesperson would need the names of papers you want, and whether you want a certain number of copies of the same issue or a running subscription for X months.

The more precise and easy-to-understand these information requirements are, the more easily you'll buy their services. You could simply put the required info in a text message to either of the above businesspeople, and they would give you exactly what you expected.

These rules and requirements make up the *API* for these services. With a well-thought-out API, the service provider becomes like a black box – you put in a query and get the right response every time.

APIs are essential in modern software design.

Say you want to build a mobile app that checks the weather forecast for the day and tells you before you leave for work if you should carry an umbrella/warm jacket etc.

Naturally, this software needs to get weather information from somewhere to work. The most convenient way to get this critical "ingredient" would be if a weather company *already* provided that information as a service through a web API. If that exists, a simple solution to build your app would be to simply send a query to that weather company through their API, say at 8 am every day, and get the day's weather information as a response.

If this service is not free, you may have to pay the weather company beforehand and they may charge you based on how often you query their API, etc.

Often in technical discussions, the API is synonymous with the service itself. Now – if the weather company *does not* offer an easy-to-use web API, things get complicated. You must find another way to get weather information.

The possibilities are many, and they range from something simple such as automatically "scraping" the weather company's website (= writing code that can read a webpage online and extract information without their explicit permission) or a more manual process where a human inputs the forecast into a web form every morning and your app gets it from there.

The latter (with manual input) becomes a more expensive and complex project than the former.

Consider Target or Walmart – the fact that you can buy something online and then pick it up at a store. How would you design that system, and what kind of manual effort would go into making these transactions successful? You need the software system to know exactly what's in stock across all the stores, keep this info updated on the back-end, etc.

If your application needs to run on a Mars rover and tell the weather there, you can't even rely on web-based APIs anymore – you have to write code that uses the robot's environment sensors to figure out the forecast by itself.

A basic web-based weather API is actually free of cost these days. You can easily build an app for yourself that checks the weather on the internet. However, if your app will be used by millions of people every week, you have to pay the company for such large volumes of requests.

Another example is online payments. Say you want your apps to accept money online through all kinds of methods all over the world (credit cards, digital wallets, bank accounts, etc.). Writing software for this from scratch would require massive levels of effort to build partnerships with a variety of domestic and international stakeholders, making sure the software is secure, fraud-proof, and so on. Most companies don't want to build the entire thing themselves, though some do. Naturally, this kind of API is not free. One such company is Stripe, currently worth almost a hundred billion dollars. They charge you a small fee on each transaction that uses their API.

In Chapter Eight, we'll discuss how APIs are not just external but also very important *internally* within tech companies.

**Summary:**

There's a division of labor at every level in the software world – from reusing lines of code someone else has already written, to reusing large software programs, to entire systems and industries. Engineers have created endless tools, frameworks, and best practices to make this global "economy" of software work better and continue to take advantage of new technology to try new things.

———◆———

# Now let's exercise our intuition around system design.

(This is the most important part of this chapter, but it's just a quick drill to kick things off. We'll revisit this later throughout the book.)

A food business has to consider things such as the following:

- What's on the menu

- The target customers and their preferences

- The source of ingredients, their price, and quality

- Packaging and delivery mode of the food prepared

- Efficiency and scalability of the kitchen

- Costs of producing the food and delivering it to the customer

Depending on the variations in such factors, your food business could vary widely. It could look like a McDonald's joint, a 3 Michelin-starred sushi restaurant, an ice cream van, or a factory that only makes soy sauce.

Same for software/hardware. Let's ask ourselves some questions; this won't be an all-inclusive list, but it will get us running.

**What does the software need to accomplish?**

Does it control an industrial robot, a spreadsheet application like Microsoft Excel, or a video-conferencing app like Skype? What is its "job"?

### Who are your customers and what do they care about?

Your answer to this question will dictate not only the fate of your entire business but also your technical strategy. For example:

- Software that controls a robot surgeon would need to focus on sharp precision and low delay time between calculations, movements, and so on, but doesn't need to have a cute user interface. Therefore, you would ideally want the critical data processing to happen directly on the robot and not on a server elsewhere on the internet because saving even microseconds of lag time is essential.

- A computer game for 5-year-old munchkins would 100% need more effort on the cute interface and engaging visual elements than on precision control and lag time.

- When your internet speed is poor, Netflix tries its best to automatically reduce the video quality instead of pausing play altogether. This is because *they believe* that you care slightly more about being able to watch something uninterrupted than about constant high-definition quality. They designed their system to reflect this belief. YouTube, on the other hand doesn't constantly adjust the video quality in general, but only once at the beginning of a video.

This also helps you decide which features you will build *first*. Since you likely have limited time and resources, you'll have to determine whether your customers will tolerate the absence of certain features (or the presence of certain flaws) as long as they are still getting a great deal overall. This clarity will help you prioritize projects and manage your team better. (More on this in Chapter Four.)

Be a student of your trade, remember?

### What kinds of services or information does the software need to do its job?

Does it need to tell the weather, know about a traveler's hotel bookings, the latest stock prices, or someone's bank balance? And how does your software get that information? Do you generate it yourself, or get it from customers, or it's available easily on the internet, or do you have to form your own digital partnerships with large corporations around the world to get it?

A lot of people assume that an engineer building an app can wave a magic wand and all the desired information will appear on the screen. At the time of writing this book, that magic wand is still in development. The information in your software has to come from somewhere.

**Packaging and distribution.**

Your food business could serve ready-to-eat meals on tables and chairs, or deliver the food to be unpacked at home, or even deliver a meal kit that the customer will use to prepare food on their own.

Remember how Netflix didn't start streaming movies until they knew most of their customers would have fast internet? They stuck to eCommerce (and used DVDs for packaging and delivering the movie data) for many years.

Similarly, you will have to decide which channel would work best for your own customers. Another question to ponder is: Should your app be completely offline with no internet required (like my phone's camera app), or completely online (online multiplayer games fall into this bucket), or a hybrid of both (an app that can be used completely offline but can also connect to the internet)?

**What are the capabilities of the device/computer on which your software program will run?**

Your software may require a certain amount of processing power, memory, a certain operating system, or other physical resources to run. You need to make sure that whatever app you're building will work well on the devices they're intended to run on.

A Mars Rover cannot (yet) connect with the internet directly and has very limited features – wheels, sensors, and some other tools that its software needs to control. On the other hand, Microsoft Paint can access inputs from a mouse and keyboard. A video-conferencing app needs access to speakers, a microphone, a camera, and a high-speed internet connection on your device.

This probably sounds too obvious, but a lot of people fail to take this into account. Ask yourself which devices or platforms you are building for and why.

**Cost**

Self-explanatory. Economics is the overriding factor. You can't go building the Great Wall of China with an Eiffel Tower budget. (More on this in Chapter Four.)

The combination of concepts like APIs and services, programming frameworks, and "stacks" have made modern software engineering much easier than it was in the last century, and at the same time more complex!

The greater the variety of ingredients, techniques, and equipment you have available, the easier it is to make simpler meals – and this keeps raising customer expectations of what a meal should be. Today's engineers are more like conductors of mini-orchestras than skilled piano or flute players. And the concerts just keep getting bigger.

Understanding technology always begins with understanding the world you live in.

Congratulations, you've reached the end of this chapter! Phew. It's a pretty big deal. But guess what – this was just a quick glimpse of what you're going to learn.

————◆————

*P.S.* While I'm a fan of Thai Curry with rice, I absolutely adore Japanese Curry with *udon* noodles. Even though Japanese food tends to be "light" in general, their curry is one of the few foods with a very rich texture and a strong flavor profile. And I'm Indian, so you know I'm serious. Also, speaking of Japanese food, I've observed that sun-dried tomatoes go surprisingly well in sushi rolls.

*P.P.S.* This is coming a bit late, but maybe I should apologize for my inconsistent spelling – due to my mixed educational background, I switch unpredictably between British and American English. Whenever my spell-check software finds a conflict in my writing (such as "color" vs "colour"), instead of "correcting" it, I choose the nationality of the word on a whim in the moment. I do wonder if I'm more inclined to choose the British spelling when I feel grumpy or sarcastic, but have never tried to confirm this.

**Artist: Ammie Govers (USA)**

*Scan the (hidden) QR code in this artwork for special bonus content.*

# *The Four Magic Words*

I often get questions like these:

"I need to hire a rockstar developer/CTO immediately. But how do I properly interview candidates? I have no way of knowing if they're good at what they do or even whether they're the right choice for my company. All I have to go on is their reputation from working at BigTech XYZ or ABC and that their peers really love them."

Or, "I'm completely dependent on my CTO for all the tech decisions. How do I know if they're telling me the truth? And how do I know if they're making the right decision?"

In your journey as an entrepreneur or leader, you'll naturally often find yourself in a position where you're hiring a technical expert in a domain where you have zero experience. You would personally have no idea how to judge how good they really are or whether they're the right person for *your team*. It could be an engineer/CTO, but the same may apply to finance, legal counsel, manufacturing operations, etc.

Often while hiring, to be "safe," you may be tempted to fall back on other people's opinions. For example,

1. You hire them because their CV is lined with brand names, and they showed interest in working with you, so "they must be right for me." (Unfortunately, if they turn out not to be, neither Google nor Facebook will owe you an apology.)

2. "My mentor/investor recommended them," "my friend couldn't stop praising them," "they've worked at a similar company as the one I'm trying to build," etc etc etc. While all these are great plus points, they're still secondary factors.)

3. You ask a third-party expert to interview them on your behalf. Or, you go online and look up things like "interview questions for X role." Then you quiz them and see how well they do, based on whatever rubric you found online.

(This might be a good start, but may not filter the right candidates for *your* team.)

All these approaches make it seem like you're collecting a "second opinion" but are really just indirect ways of relegating the critical judgment to someone else.

Managing experts can also be quite delicate. You'd delegate a lot of authority and autonomy to this person but have no way of really *managing* them. By meeting and discussing things with them regularly, you'd get the illusion that you're closely collaborating, but as a matter of fact you'd still mostly watch them do their stuff from a distance — hoping that you're on the same page, but not be able to intelligently discuss their work (because when you do so, you get confused by all the jargon), etc.

Although becoming more tech-fluent will help you delegate authority with more confidence, it won't automatically negate the gulf in knowledge between you. Due to this communication gap, you could someday get a growing feeling that "something's not right," and the stress and anxiety can chip away at your trustful professional relationship.

So what do you do?

There is a way to *enhance* trust and communication, in a gentle and humble way that deflates any chance of conflict or distrust while still being able to ask blunt questions comfortably without hesitation.

*Four magic words* which will almost single-handedly ensure that you have a healthy long-term partnership:

***"Can you teach me...?"***

Just explicitly ask them to educate you about whatever it is they're doing or want to do. And they should have the ability and patience to explain to you what they're doing and why they're doing it, in simple words you can understand.

Notice that this is the same trick that Larry Page used with Sebastian Thrun in the story from Chapter Two — when he was trying to convince Thrun to join his dream self-driving car project. Often, just by humbly asking a person to explain their thought process, you can identify weak points in their decisions, contribute your own ideas and gain influence without creating animosity.

I also use this trick as my number one "filtering method" for experts. For me to work with them, they have to have the **Heart of a Teacher.**

If they're excited to teach you, if they add value to you and make you better at managing them every single time you discuss their work, then it's a positive sign.

If an expert does not have the heart of a teacher (if you're not sure, they don't), don't make them your trusted expert. The best players don't necessarily make the best coaches! Only work with non-teachers if you know enough about the subject yourself to not require any teaching or if they'll be in a capacity where you won't directly manage them.

There are other good reasons for this:

1. If someone loves teaching and is good at it, they're usually very competent and have a fairly deep understanding of their field. You can easily separate the bullshitters from the real deal.

2. Someone with this attitude will also be a good coach and manager, thus helping you build a team with a healthy culture.

3. They're usually proactive with communication — if they love teaching, they'll be excited to tell you about whatever it is they're working on.

If anything, I find it quite obvious that *it's the expert's job to educate the non-expert.* But I still see many entrepreneurs tolerate their CTO subtly talking down to them while struggling to explain stuff. Don't let anyone do that to you. You have a right to DEMAND education.

So look for the "heart of a teacher." You'll thank yourself for it.

Chapter Four

# The FBI's $700M Mistake

After the 9/11 attacks, it was shockingly revealed that the United States Federal Bureau of Investigation (FBI) already had information that easily could have prevented the attacks. It was just sitting there, but they didn't see it on time.

The biggest reason for this was also surprising to everybody — except to those *inside* the FBI. It was a technology issue.

Imagine you're an FBI agent trying to uncover a complex terrorist plot. You want to find out what connections different suspects might have across multiple cases and link together pieces of information from around the country. By closely following the various threads of evidence and information, you can figure out a story of what's going on.

In 2001, these things were quite hard to do. The FBI still mainly used the type of paperwork and file cabinets they'd used since the 1920s when they first began chasing gangsters. In the 1990s, an agent named Larry Depew ran an extensive undercover operation on both Russian mobsters and the Italian mafia for 2.5 years, but even after all the wiretapping and surveillance, they still didn't have a solid case. Then one day, Depew found out that one of his colleagues had a briefcase full of information about the entire back-end operations and financial organization of the crime syndicates he was investigating. It had been sitting there since *1989*, right under his nose, and he had been running around doing risky operations for years looking for information the FBI already had. It became the central piece of evidence that finally enabled them to win.

Without a well-designed, searchable database with easy-to-use software, a large organization like the FBI couldn't really know what it knew. Looking through thousands of paper case files was impossible, so they couldn't link or share information between investigations.

They did have a few computers, but with *1980s technology*. These computers had a database system called the "Automated Case Support," (ACS) which had old green screens that you had to type commands into, and it couldn't display graphics or pictures — they had to print out every document they wanted to see. They couldn't simply type in a name or some keywords and quickly see all the related information — they had to type in complicated functions to do different types of queries. Uploading a single document took 12 steps.

ACS was very hard to use for everyone except the most dedicated, computer-savvy agents who also had the patience of a Himalayan hermit (one of them being Robert Hanssen, a double agent working for the USSR, who used ACS to find and leak top-secret information to the KGB, as well as to check if anyone at the FBI was investigating him).

Naturally, since investigations are time-sensitive, many agents gave up on the frustrating computers and simply did things on paper, the old-school way. Instead of email, most agents used a fax machine or sent CDs and floppy disks through FedEx.

Under heavy criticism, the FBI decided to modernize its information systems. This contract was given to the "Science Applications International Corporation" (SAIC). At first, they started on a relatively small project in June 2001, named the "Virtual Case File" (VCF). The goal was simply to put a web-based front-end to ACS so that agents could access it on a PC with a slightly more intuitive interface.

After 9/11, they decided to go above and beyond. Emotions were running high across the USA, and the government wanted to show everyone that they were sparing no effort or expense. They decided that VCF wouldn't simply be a web front-end to replace the green screens; it would replace all prior systems altogether, including ACS, and migrate its data to a fresh Oracle database. They would create a brand-new system for the FBI from scratch, including new computers and networking hardware — effectively revolutionizing their technology.

In January 2002, four months after the terrorist attack, the FBI asked Congress for $70M to accelerate the timelines. They got $78M instead. (Lucky for SAIC — the 9/11 attacks gave a boost to their business overall; they soon clocked $7 billion in revenue.)

Unfortunately, despite the good intentions, what followed was one disastrous project after another (more on this later), costing hundreds of millions of dollars of American taxpayers' money. Until 2012, ten years after the World Trade Center collapsed, FBI agents were still at the mercy of paper trails and PCs running decades-old software.

———◆———

Chapter Three helped us brush up on some of the fundamentals. In the following few chapters, we'll go deeper into databases, cybersecurity, scalability, machine learning, and other things.

But before we go there, it's important to realize that making the right *technical decisions* is only 20 percent of engineering. The other 80 percent is about planning, management, and execution — and that is the focus of this all-important chapter.

Building a company is a process of three things happening at the same time:

* *Creation* – creating products and systems to reach the desired goal,

* *Information gathering* – figuring out what the market wants, and

* *Problem-solving* – getting over obstacles that get in the way of the other two

Moreover, it is a resource-intensive process. It constantly costs you time, money, and precious human resources.

The first, and the most significant part of this job, is managing risk. **You are a risk ecologist.**

You want to mitigate the risk that you are:

* Making something that nobody wants,

* Making something that breaks or doesn't work as it's supposed to,

* Wasting or running out of time, money, or resources before reaching the goal

Most new companies fail for one or more of the above reasons. Even if you raise more money than you know what to do with (not recommended, but congrats), it's still a game of juggling multiple glass balls.

From an engineering standpoint, the key step is *choosing or creating a development process that aligns with your business goals.* Every business is different and has a different risk profile, so no one approach or philosophy works perfectly for all. You'll have to craft your own.

Furthermore, being a "non-technical" entrepreneur, you'll probably spend most of your time on responsibilities like sales, marketing, finance, etc., and not supervising developers. So by instinct, they probably won't see you as *their manager* even if you're the CEO. They'll usually reserve that for the CTO, or the tech lead, or whoever is the senior-most developer on the team. They'll be inclined to see you instead as an internal customer, or at most a project coordinator.

This is where the lines get even more blurrier. When the team is making a big, strategic technical decision, a good tech team will usually want to insist that you leave the matter in their hands. You have to know when to let them do their thing, and when to interrupt and assert yourself without coming across as a micromanager. In the same vein, when you make a decision about which engineering team gets how much budget, how do you explain your reasoning convincingly?

There's the second big part of your job: **managing human psychology and energy.**

Any technical plan or even business strategy which conveniently forgets the pitfalls of *human nature* is nothing more than a fairy tale, and a bad one at that. This is a critical but often overlooked fact in every field, whether you're an entrepreneur, a sporting team captain, or a military general.

All these non-technical aspects of engineering can make or break your company, and are necessary in order for you to be considered tech-fluent. When there are no hard rules or directions to follow, it helps to have "north stars" and first principles to rely on instead.

These challenges were also faced by the FBI agents while navigating their technology transformation, so in this chapter, we'll dissect their case study in more detail and glean lessons.

By the way, although the full story is more entertaining than an Agatha Christie mystery novel, I'm not here to mock the FBI or anything. I'm an educator, not a clickbait news reporter. We're only using their story because fortunately, all the related information is publicly available, which is rarely possible with private-sector failures.

## "Shooting From The Hip"

Let's go back to our story of the FBI being *fed up* with their technology situation (that was a good pun and you know it). We'll look at the red flags along the way – though there are too many to list – that led to a complete breakdown of good engineering practices, and discuss what could have been done.

The leadership wanted a new case management software as quickly as possible, so SAIC was asked to build and release an entirely new system within 22 months flat. They also decided to write the whole software *from scratch* instead of modifying commercial off-the-shelf software that already existed. The timeline was so aggressive that none of the contracts even mentioned any project milestones or schedules. All they had was a final delivery date. Moreover, the contracts said that the FBI would even pay for any cost overruns. (I'm positive SAIC's salespeople loved that one.)

To make things even faster, they made another extreme decision: they would deploy VCF in one swift move all at once, called a *flash cut* or *big bang adoption*. Essentially, they would shut down ACS on the day of deployment and turn on VCF immediately, with no transition phase in between. This would be a permanent change. The new system had to work perfectly from day one because if it didn't, too bad — there was no way to go back to ACS. It was hit or miss.

Most of the FBI's technology talent had been leaving the agency to work in the private sector for years, so they placed Agent Larry Depew, who previously had been hunting down mobs and mafia members, as the I.T. project manager. He was passionate about technology and knew how to write code. This was the very first I.T. project he had ever managed.

For the first six months, the teams met in two-week sessions where FBI agents would explain to SAIC engineers on a whiteboard how the internal investigative procedures worked, how they wanted cases to be handled, etc. The agents would rattle off ideas about exactly what functionality they wanted, how they wanted the layout to look, how the interface had to work — they wanted certain things on the left side, a logo here, a button there in X color, etc. The result? *Eight hundred pages* of detailed requirements.

With the deadline and deliverables in hand, SAIC teams started shipping code. To finish the job faster, they divided the engineering effort into eight different teams working in parallel, following an iterative development cycle where each team would constantly ship features and get feedback from the customer.

Every two weeks, SAIC would code up and send a version of the software to the FBI to review. The agents would ask for changes of various kinds, ranging from the cosmetic (move this button from here to there) to the procedural (add a new core function that affects all eight development teams), so the project's scope and "requirements" changed on a weekly basis. Whatever the FBI asked for, SAIC would okay it, put it on the bill, and get back to work.

In July 2002, Sherry Higgins, the I.T. program manager, gave a glowing Powerpoint presentation to the U.S. Senate about how wonderful VCF was going to be, and that it would be delivered by the agreed deadline 18 months later. The Senate was impressed, even gushing over Higgins' humor and "Southern charm." Everything seemed to be going well.

But in October 2002, out of the blue, a whistleblower emerged. Matthew Patton, a SAIC security engineer who had previously worked at the Pentagon, went online to describe the "crippling mismanagement" of a project that was critical to national security.

He revealed that SAIC had two hundred engineers where only a couple dozen were necessary, each doing superficial "make work." The FBI was rattling off new software requirements like an all-you-can-eat buffet and were willing to pay anything to get what they wanted, so in Patton's words, SAIC had adopted an attitude of "it's other people's money, so we'll burn it whichever way we want to." And because every engineer was working on their own little piece, the system as a whole was also riddled with cybersecurity loopholes. Nobody seemed to care.

Patton had repeatedly brought up the issue with his managers, but they asked him to calm down and be a "team player." After he blew the whistle, instead of his pleas being tended to, he was seen as a disruptor, "chronic complainer," and security risk. He was visited by two FBI agents claiming that he had revealed national secrets on the internet, (which I presume was not a fun meeting) and was removed from the project.

But he was right, and by December 2002, the project was behind schedule. To "accelerate" it, the FBI asked Congress for more funding — and got *$123M*.

The extra money only prolonged the same story. Over the next year, the more code SAIC shipped, the more change requests they received from the FBI, and the more the project's scope evolved — even after 25% of the software had already been built! Imagine a house that's 25% constructed, and you're still making changes to the blueprint.

Delivery schedules kept slipping, the tension between the FBI and SAIC mounted, and there was a lot of finger-pointing on both sides. Meanwhile, *three different CIOs* would join and leave the FBI in quick succession in 2003 alone.

Finally, a month before the December 2003 delivery, the newest CIO, Zalmai Azmi, asked to demo the VCF system that had been built so far. It actually looked very impressive — all the layouts and functionalities were mostly as the FBI agents had wanted. But then he asked about the error rate, or the "software problem reports" (SPRs). Turns out, there were hundreds of critical errors, and new bugs were still being reported. The software was essentially glossy on the outside, dead on the inside.

An arbitrator was called in from the National Research Council (NRC). It was a team of independent scientists and engineers from universities and tech companies around the country, whom Robert Mueller, the FBI director affectionately called "the Graybeards." The Graybeards concluded three main things:

1.   Both sides were at fault, but mostly it was SAIC.

2.   The project had been poorly planned from the very beginning. And,

3.   The project was probably going to fail.

The biggest threat they saw was the planned flash cutover, which they said would be "mission-disruptive" and must not happen at any cost. One of them even joked that they were planning to go on a crime spree the day after VCF would launch, because it would unquestionably put the FBI out of business.

But in March 2004, Mueller was still optimistic and promised Congress that VCF would be working flawlessly by summer. Smelling opportunity in urgency again, SAIC asked for $50M to get the system working by summer – as if in ransom. The FBI negotiated it down to $16M.

To try and salvage the project, CIO Azmi decided to take matters into his own hands. He took a team of 120 SAIC engineers and put them on a separate track. He became heavily involved and set a strict development schedule with clearly defined milestones. He would meet his project manager every morning at 8:15am sharp, and receive an end-of-day status report at 10pm the same night.

But although this experiment was succeeding, the overall VCF project was already destined for the grave. Every external reviewer had said that it should be scrapped altogether instead of being "saved," so that's what they did. Talks were already underway for yet another project, auspiciously titled "Sentinel," which would replace VCF altogether.

The entire VCF project, with its *700,000 lines of code*, was thrown into the bin. They had lost $170M. Sentinel started in 2006 with a fresh $425M budget, scheduled for delivery in 2009. This time, the contract went to Lockheed Martin. SAIC would not be involved.

But history has a funny tendency to repeat itself. By 2008, the Sentinel project was also constantly missing deadlines and showing signs of going out of hand. The FBI hired a new CIO and CTO from the private sector (both formerly I.T. executives at Lehman Brothers, which had recently collapsed), who were now given a budget of $451M.

The 2009 deadline came and flew by. In 2010, another external audit from MITRE Corporation brought devastating news: Sentinel would take *six more years* and much more money. The new CIO decided to take back control from prime contractor Lockheed – just as Azmi had done previously with SAIC – and enforced an Agile methodology, building in two-week sprints to develop it faster.

With this, they were able to complete and deploy Sentinel in 2012. *Finally.* Sentinel won many awards for its success (most notably from the FBI itself) and was hailed as a hallmark of technical innovation in the government.

Ideally, by this point, we would want everyone to live happily ever after, but the story has a climax.

In 2014, two years after Sentinel's deployment, a survey of FBI agents by the Inspector General revealed new shocking revelations: while it was easy to use and had a nice user interface, many agents complained that Sentinel's search functionality was even *worse* in quality than the green screen ACS systems they had been trying to replace for the last 14 years! In fact, the system effectively *increased* the administrative burden on many agents, leaving them less time than before to perform investigative activities.

Moreover, it turned out that Sentinel had cost much more than its official price tag. Along the journey to build iteratively, they had left many "loose ends." Tidying these loose ends alone would cost additional tens of millions of dollars, and these bills trickled in for years.

In some ways, while trying to leap from the Bronze Age to the Digital Age, the FBI spent the better part of a billion dollars regressing back to the Stone Age instead.

# The Post Mortem

It's easy to look back in hindsight at someone else's failures and point out all the things they did wrong. It's also unlikely that you and I would never make any of these mistakes — it happens to the best of us.

Moreover, some of the decisions weren't wrong in isolation – they were wrong in that context. The same decision might be the right thing to do in a different project. Therefore, simply telling you "not to do that" without knowing whether it applies to *your* specific context would be bad advice, and make me a terrible teacher. The goal of this *technical fluency* journey is to empower you to look at your own situation and make sense of what is needed, not to give you a list of fool-proof commandments. There are no fool-proof commandments.

For both of these reasons, instead of nitpicking the story, we will learn about some first principles and look at the red flags from that perspective instead. By understanding these concepts, you'll be much further on your way to manage projects successfully than by following an arbitrary list of dos and don'ts.

As you read through this section, remember that the question we're trying to answer is *"how do you create a development plan that works best for your business or engineering project?"*

In the software industry, you'll often hear phrases like "agile," "waterfall," "lean startup," and "minimum viable product" being thrown around, as well as adages like "if you're not embarrassed by the first version of your product, you didn't release it early enough." The problem with labels and blanket statements is that everyone you'll meet will have a different interpretation. I encourage you to stay away from the semantics and *think from first principles* instead—which we'll discuss next.

## Making Friends With Risk

Suppose you're a home cooking enthusiast trying to come up with a new *caviar* dish.

You have high expectations. You're tempted to try out as many flavors and combinations as you can. But caviar is an expensive ingredient, so you don't want to waste it doing too many experiments — you want to be more thoughtful about what you're trying and why. But still, in the worst case, it's just that the recipe tastes bad. It's not a life-changing result, no big deal (unless the ingredient in question was Japanese *fugu* fish which is lethally poisonous if not prepared properly).

In short: it's *expensive* to test, but *low* in risk.

On the other hand, say you're a Michelin 3-star chef and want to introduce a new *egg* recipe. The stakes are much higher – if you serve an underwhelming omelette to an undercover food critic, you might get a nasty article written about you. At worst, if you lost a Michelin star or two, it could mean shutting down the restaurant. Luckily, even if you buy high-quality eggs, they're still a cheap ingredient. For you, it's almost worth burning a hundred eggs in a hundred ways until the final dish befits your reputation!

*Inexpensive to test, but high in risk.*

So here's the concept: choosing the right *development process* for anything, whether it's a new recipe, a water gun for toddlers, the FBI virtual case file system, or a nuclear submarine, is governed by two overarching factors:

1. The risk involved if it doesn't succeed

2. How much it costs to do testing

In general, you want to test things as early as possible, as often as possible. *Test Early, Test Often.* And you always want to choose the test that is both cheaper *and* less risky if it fails.

Now the question arises: *what ARE we testing, exactly?*

In engineering, there are two types of tests. The first type tests WHAT you should be doing and whether it's worth doing in the first place. The second type tests the different ways for HOW it should be done.

In technical terms, testing the "how" is called **verification** (verifying that what you built works as *you* wanted it), and testing the "what" is called **validation** (validating the overall premise that what you've built is even useful in the first place).

A lot of people confuse these two. They're looking for the best path to scale the mountain, without even being sure of which mountain they're trying to climb.

## Your Validation Strategy

To start with the WHAT, you must identify your biggest risk factors, which can *make or break the business,* and then do tests that tell you as early as you can if you're going in the right direction or not. One good way to see it is trying to test your most *fundamental assumptions* as soon as possible.

A validation test can involve something as simple as surveying 100 strangers on the street, doing simulations on a whiteboard, or building a million-dollar prototype.

For Dropbox, Drew Houston made a 3-minute demo video describing what the product would *eventually* do — before even building it — and asked any interested people to sign up with their email on a waitlist. When the waitlist exploded to over 75,000 people, he knew the project had passed the very first validation test, which was that people wanted the product.

For Zoom, founder Eric Yuan's big assumption was that *enterprises* badly needed a video conferencing app that was easier to use than Skype or Webex. What's traditionally a good way to validate this idea? Customer interviews. But these can be deceptive – people don't often know what they want, until you show them what's possible! Many great ideas, such as Henry Ford's automobile, Steve Jobs' iPhone, or even the humble sticky-notes, wouldn't have passed the traditional "customer interview."

In Zoom's case, Yuan took a big leap — he started the company with forty engineers, spent eighteen months crafting the product, and then launched a beta version that directly got Stanford University as its first client.

In general, the best validation for such ideas is to put a *prototype* in the hands of your target customers and see how they like it.

Prototypes are of various kinds – ranging from quick and dirty to highly functional. This is called *fidelity*. An example of a *low-fidelity* prototype is the sketch of an app's interface on a whiteboard. A *high-fidelity* prototype is as close to the real product as possible – such as coding up a version of the app that actually works and can be used.

No matter the level of fidelity, a prototype is still a "test" – so the choice of how much fidelity you need still depend on the risks and costs associated with it!

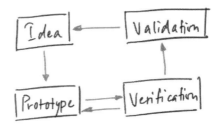

Idea -> Prototype <-> Verify Prototype -> Validate Idea

When building a new skateboard, you know that the worst that happens is someone falling from it. It is definitely a safety issue, but not too much. It's also cheap to craft a new skateboard in your garage and take it for a spin. So you'd want to skip the low-fidelity prototypes (like elaborate designs on paper) and instead churn out a high-fidelity, working skateboard every week until you arrive at the perfect design.

Developing a new *passenger airplane?* It's incredibly expensive to build a *single* real, high-fidelity prototype, and the risks involved in its failure are also huge. You'd spend a lot more time iterating at the "whiteboard stage," making sure the low-fidelity design is perfect before you fold a single sheet of metal. You would simulate and test your theories and designs on a computer, then test with a small *miniature* prototype in an air tunnel (still quite low-fidelity), and so on.

I have a friend whose company is actually building autonomous cargo planes. Another friend is building advanced semiconductor chips for AI applications. Both of them, by nature of their business, have to spend (and raise) $100M over several years, and go through dozens of smaller milestones and tests before they can ship a single high-fidelity prototype! By necessity, much of their efforts go into refining their ideas and testing their assumptions at a very low level of fidelity.

Most modern software development is about going from one high-fidelity, working prototype to another. Instead of "wasting time" with low-fidelity tests, you ship a working version of the software so you can actually observe people using your product in the real world, thus getting the most objective feedback possible. In theory, this is great! Build fast, ship fast, fail fast, try again.

Recall that SAIC did something similar for the FBI. They took the requirements, created eight teams of developers, and got to coding. They also got very frequent feedback and "change requests" from the agents. So in spite of following the above principles, why did things go wrong?

That brings us to the next principle.

But before we go there, a quick summary: whatever the level of fidelity, a prototype is still a kind of "validation test." In principle, its goal is no different from doing a survey or simulation – to tell you WHAT you should be building and whether it is worth building.

Take a break to review what you've learned.

## Technical Architecture

Let me pose a very basic question: why do we need to create a "blueprint" when we're building a house, but it's not considered helpful when building igloos in the snow or sandcastles on the beach?

Or, have you ever played with large Lego kits, such as the ones for building a complete *Millennium Falcon* spaceship? Why do those kits come with detailed blueprints? (FYI, I never played with those kits as a kid because my parents refused to buy them. Just sharing some "childhood trauma" with you; don't mind me, thanks for listening.)

The reason for a blueprint is, quite intuitively, *complexity*. In a house, the interior design, the plumbing, electrical wiring, and other things greatly affect each other. When you're trying to build something "complex" that has many disparate pieces that affect each other's function, you need a blueprint.

So, a quick concept here: *the greater the complexity, the more you need a detailed blueprint.*

Large software projects can have so many moving parts that they're more akin to building giant water parks than houses. For software applications, this blueprint is referred to as a technical architecture.

In the case of VCF, the official report stated that the lack of a technical architecture was the single biggest reason for the project's failure. Instead, the FBI had a mammoth 800-page requirements document with various levels of detail. It was as if an enthusiastic young couple had written a long "wishlist" for their dream house, from the color of the bedsheets in the baby's room to the ideal temperature of the toilet seat, and then let the contractors figure out the rest among themselves.

The overly specific requirements focused engineers on tiny pieces of the system, with nobody knowing how they would be *integrated* into a functioning whole – creating deep "cracks" in the product codebase which could not be filled, and lots of "technical debt" (things which improve the quality of the work, but which you have to leave unfinished because you're under a deadline) piling up.

This is why following an iterative "ship fast" development strategy actually had a negative effect on the VCF project. Recall the FBI's endless stream of change requests whenever they saw a version of whatever SAIC shipped. When you don't have a strong architecture, you can't grasp the seriousness of different types of changes to requirements. Asking to change the flooring is very different from asking to move a bathroom from one corner of the house to another. Whenever you make a change that affects the underlying blueprint (i.e. technical architecture), you greatly delay the project and increase the costs involved.

A good technical architecture also helps you make decisions about which parts of the solution you will need to build from scratch and which ones you can buy off-the-shelf from the market. Of course, there's nothing stopping you from building everything from scratch, but you have to be realistic given the timelines you're looking at. You wouldn't be able to ascertain this just from reading this book, but I can tell you that building a software system as large and complex as VCF is not unlike building a standalone, mature enterprise software company. To accomplish that within less than two years, writing every line of code from scratch instead of modifying commercially available software is quite a tall order! The FBI later alleged that SAIC urged them into this plan of doing everything from scratch, which of course the latter denied.

As a leader, you'll often tackle "build vs buy" decisions. Most smartly-run I.T. organizations have an "enterprise architecture" to guide all decisions about how things will work, how different parts of the system will connect and operate with each other, what software and hardware they'll invest in, etc. (In Chapter Eight, we will learn how to actually create a solid technical architecture.)

A subtle factor that compounded the chaos was that the project managers and technical leadership at the FBI constantly changed throughout the project. (Going back to the young-couple-with-house-wishlist analogy, imagine if one or both the spouses also kept changing throughout the project.)

Upon hearing the story above, people usually give me widely different types of reactions. Some love to think that people working in the government are dumb and lazy by default. Others point the finger at the engineering contractors, saying that they had a broken ethical compass.

I'm not looking for lawsuits here, and honestly, I've more or less given up trying to answer the age-old question of "why people do what they do." (Ask someone who lives in a cave meditating in the Himalayas or something, maybe he would tell you.)

I submit to you the last section of this chapter.

## Engineering Culture: The Hidden Force

When I was training to be a systems engineer, most of my instructors and peers came from the aerospace and defense industries. They worked at federal agencies like NASA or big U.S. defense contractors like Lockheed Martin and Raytheon.

For most of them, "tech" meant rocket jet propulsion, wireless communication systems, and nuclear warheads, not smartphone widgets. Their way of thinking was different from most software engineers I know. Some of them even looked down on Silicon Valley software developers, saying that they're not real engineers. (*Shrug*)

I can somewhat empathize. They come from a very different "culture" where the expectations and incentives were quite different. As we saw earlier in the chapter, such engineers are used to BIG, expensive projects. The margin for error is tiny, and the risks astronomical. They do a *lot* of planning and drown in a lot of paperwork before they start building anything, and have no urge to "ship things quickly."

On the other hand, in many software companies that follow an "agile" methodology, engineers develop in strict "sprints" — shipping a working version of the product every 2-4 weeks and participating in daily check-in meetings to discuss progress. In aerospace terms, it's akin to five-year-olds building toys with clay. Contrary to what happens in many software companies these days, I've never met an old-school software developer who would tell their program manager things like, "oh yeah, I tested the code once, it should be alright."

Jokes aside, the "traditional" engineering culture is not without flaws. It has a dark side.

In 1986 on a cold January morning, NASA faced its most tragic disaster yet. The space shuttle *Challenger* was scheduled to fly early in the day. While in space, the crew was going to study Haley's Comet, which wouldn't appear again for another 75 years. Millions of people worldwide were watching live on TV, and U.S. President Ronald Reagan had already prepared a speech to applaud the successful launch afterward. Unfortunately, he would give a very different speech. Seventy-three seconds into the flight, the shuttle burst into flames, killing the entire team of astronauts on board.

During investigations afterward, something astounding was revealed.

Only a few hours before the launch, a team of very angry and depressed engineers, who worked for one of NASA's biggest subcontractors, had spent all night in a heated debate with their managers and the customer team at NASA. They insisted that the launch be aborted, saying that due to the cold temperatures that day, a design flaw would cause the shuttle to break apart. They pleaded for the launch to wait for a warmer day.

But given the circumstances, there was tremendous pressure from their managers and from NASA — the whole world was watching. So the engineering managers made them go along with the group and let the launch happen as planned. Later, after the tragedy occurred, they tried to cover it up. When the truth came out, the whistleblower engineers got demoted and cut off from space work, shunned by their colleagues and managers for hurting the company's public relations, and eventually had to quit. Due to the PTSD, they suffered from severe headaches, depression, and insomnia.

A similar problem repeated itself in 1998 and caused NASA's two Mars surveyor spacecraft to fail. These disasters were traumatic for everyone involved, but they have become infamous case studies in project management and team culture — not engineering. Large projects like these are like gigantic sailing ships. Once it's going at full speed, it's tough to make it suddenly change course like a speedboat. The sheer momentum and collective groupthink are so powerful that nobody wants to hear you say, "hey I know we've spent a lot of time and money on this, but I think we may need to change the plan because we just realized this might not work." People can feel forced to go along the flow and put up a "can do" face.

Recently, *company culture* has been a cool topic, which is probably a good thing. But most people don't know how to describe it or where it comes from.

Some describe it almost as a *feeling* that's hard to put the finger on: morale, energy, camaraderie and what not. People will say it depends on the examples set by leadership, how often colleagues give each other honest feedback, how often you play board games together, and a host of other factors.

While this is a very subjective topic, here's my definition: *Culture is how people VIEW their work, themselves, and their colleagues.*

The way people *view* their work affects how they make decisions when nobody's looking. And this perspective, counter-intuitively, depends ultimately on the *incentives and mechanisms* set in place by the company.

On aggregate, people default to doing whatever they think is in their best interest to do. It's only human. No number of inspirational speeches from the "boss," outdoor team-building activities or holding hands in a circle can change a team's culture if the *fundamental nature* of their work is not aligned. This is especially true as your company scales, and employees and leadership become more distant.

Listen, I get it. We all love nothing more than to pull a list of virtuous slogans and mottos out of thin air, and put them on posters to share our supposed "beliefs" with employees. One company I know had a "credo statement" which literally said, *"Call bullshit!"* Every week, they reiterated it at the beginning of All Hands meetings to signal employees to give each other honest feedback, do the right thing, etc. Their employees did call bullshit – in Glassdoor reviews, unfortunately.

From employees' perspective, your company's "core values" aren't worth the paper they're written on. They've seen such a list at every company they've worked before, and the list always looks the same. Employees only see how things really work and create their *own* list of credos to follow. The question you should be asking instead is, "what are we incentivising people to do?"

In the FBI's software projects, the incentives were misaligned from the beginning. From signing a contract that promised additional payment for all cost overruns (creating a direct conflict of interest), to having no project milestones or schedule except a final delivery date (removing all urgency and giving teams the impression that they could "slack off"), there seemed to be a systematic breakdown of best practices.

I should clarify here that being intentional about your culture and writing down your core values is a GOOD thing! I wrote some down for my company too. But I use them mostly as a reminder to myself – so I can make decisions accordingly. I'm under no delusion that anyone else on my team cares about them as much as I do.

The key takeaway again is that you can choose the type of culture you want, but to change it, you can't rely on soft tools like rhetoric and inspirational hoo-haa. Change the structure and incentives at play instead.

———◆———

There are many other red flags and causes of failure that we could discuss, but they all stem from the factors we discussed above, and we've seen enough for now. In closing, Larry Depew, VCF's original project manager, said it best: "We wanted it really bad, and in the end it was really bad."

In Chapters Eight and Nine, we will dive deeper into some of the more tactical topics – how to write good requirements and tests, define technical architecture, etc.

Final note: I know this was a somewhat depressing/cynical chapter, but now, lighten up! The rest of the book isn't that gloomy, I promise. (Well, maybe except for the Cybersecurity chapter, but it's all in good fun.)

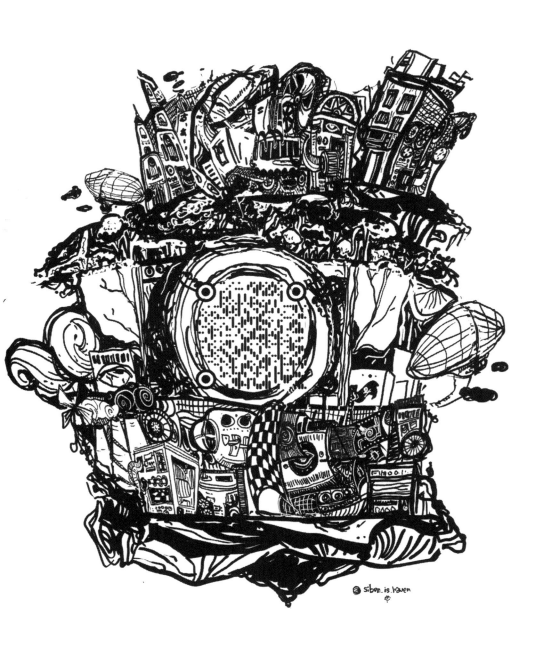

**Artist: Inan Anjum Sibun (Bangladesh)**

*Scan this artwork like a QR code for optional bonus content.*

<< Section Break >>

# *A Strange Request*

You've finished the first section of this book!

Before we move on, I have a request for you.

I've been writing online for almost a decade, and I'm still regularly surprised and inspired by the sheer diversity of people I happen to reach and hear back from. Art teachers in the Tokyo suburbs, high-profile executives on Wall Street, stay-at-home moms in the French countryside, high schoolers in Nigeria — the list continues to go beyond what I ever imagined.

It's more than likely that you and I have never met. But you are reading my words, and we are sharing this moment together. Now I ask *you* to write back to me and tell me a little about yourself! Share something about your story and your aspirations, and tell me which parts of this book were your favorite. Writing for me is a two-way communication channel, and your messages enrich my life much more than I do in return.

You're welcome to contact me via email (aman@sanpram.com) or find me on social media (my username is usually "mngrwl"). I read every message, and can't wait to hear from you.

If you include a picture or a short video to show me what life is like wherever you are, I would appreciate it even more!

# *Enter the Internet*

In this lesson, I will re-introduce you to the internet – in a way you've never been – and gain a new appreciation of how it works at a deeper level.

For example, what happens when you type a website name online and hit enter? What is the difference between "streaming" video data for hours versus sending a single email or message online? We will answer these by learning about web protocols, network layers, types of web requests, and so on.

I'd consider this lesson to be optional reading because although the following information is fascinating, it's not immediately useful or practical for you as an entrepreneur.

(This also means I *forbid* you to stop reading the book right after finishing this chapter; if that's your intention, I'd rather you skip it altogether and read the next chapter before moving on.) If you have time though, I do recommend you go through it because it is simple to understand and will enrich your technical base.

As you recall from Chapter Three, the internet is a global network of computers, and it allows computers to talk to each other. But this description doesn't create a good enough picture of what is really going on. So let's go on a fantasy-historical journey.

Say you were alive 400 years ago, living in a little hut on the outskirts of a big city, such as Edo (Tokyo) or London. I've chosen this setting to remove all traces of modern communication technology.

Your hut needs to exchange things and information with the hut right next to it.

You are neighbors, and you speak the same language, so you cut out a hole in the wall through which you can pass objects and messages to each other.

It's a very fast and elegant solution. You don't have to walk out or travel – you can use the hole like a mini-door for private communication. You also agree on some rules, such as keeping the hole covered and having to knock before opening it, for privacy reasons.

In this network of two huts, the hole is the infrastructure that allows communication. On top of that, you use a common language and agree on some protocols to make the system work efficiently and beautifully for both of you.

If you want to include more huts into this network, you would have to change things.

One way is to have a chain of holes between all the huts, so that information could pass as a relay from one hut to the next. But you all agree that this is a terrible system (who wants to spend their whole day passing objects from one hole to another and having no privacy?).

Instead, say you agree to build a central "router hut" in your community that connects to all other huts through dedicated pipes, etc. You employ some staff for this router, like in a post office.

To send anything, you send it to the router hut along with a message that states the source and destination. Now all huts can easily communicate with each other.

Thus, the infrastructure has evolved into a bigger system of a router hut with its pipes, holes, staff, and other things connecting all the huts. The language and protocols have also changed. Instead of the freeform casual language you were able to use with your neighbor, now you have to use a more standardized way to share information, so that the central hut staff can understand it and send your message forward. You now also have to declare the source and destination of each message.

This is akin to an "intranet" – a secluded local network. This network is limited to your community, and won't work for all the buildings in the city or state.

The internet is a much larger and more complex version of such a network, but the principles are the same:

Your computer needs to speak the same *language* and use standard processes agreed upon by all other computers on the internet. Instead of just one big central hut, you now have many nodes throughout this network that relay your messages to their destination.

It's still a massive, digital "postal service" sending packages from one place to another.

## The Protocols

To keep such a network running smoothly, you have to have multiple *protocols* for different aspects of the communication process. There are some for how a message is packaged and delivered, how the message should be written and interpreted, etc.

Say you wish to send an application for a new passport to the designated office. They may say,

1.  "We only receive applications via mail."

2.  "The application must be in so-and-so format."

This means there is first a protocol for how the connection will be set up, and then *another* protocol for how the messages are written. "Send an application *via email, in xyz format.*" So you have two different *layers* of protocols one after another, and you must follow *both*. Make sense?

On the internet, messages are sent in the form of "data packets." For delivering individual messages, one connection protocol is TCP/IP. It's a very secure protocol with back-and-forth checks to make sure the right parties are exchanging information.

For writing the messages sent via a TCP connection, the most popular protocol followed is called HTTP. There are other protocol alternatives to HTTP, but it's the most common one. If this is confusing again, just remember that:

*You write a request using the HTTP protocol, and send it through a connection that's set up using the TCP/IP protocol.*

Now, as I said earlier, TCP/IP is a great secure protocol. If you wanted to deliver an expensive bottle of wine to your neighbor, following a TCP/IP protocol would mean neatly packaging and delivering it with great care and confirming that they've received it.

But not every communication needs to be this careful and "slow." For instance, say you want to do video streaming and voice calls over the internet, or create an online multiplayer virtual reality Metaverse game that requires smooth motion and *low latency.* You'd prefer to use a connection protocol that allows faster transmission – even if a few data packets get lost the way. The UDP protocol is great for this – it allows you to send out data as a "stream" while sacrificing a bit of security and reliability.

Following the expensive wine example, the UDP protocol is more like filling it into small rubber balloons and quickly throwing them one after another at your neighbour's house, assuming he's ready to catch.

**IP Addresses and Domains**

With the TCP/IP protocol (most connections), computer addresses are called IP addresses, and they're in the form of 4-12 digit numbers such as 2001:4860:4860.

But it's so hard to remember all these numbers. That's why we have website names like Google.com! These are called domain names.

Recall what you learned about the internet at the beginning of the course – that when you visit Google.com, you are essentially trying to communicate with their backend servers – these are the computers you're talking to! The domain name "Google.com" simply gets converted into an IP address of the backend servers.

These messages themselves are written in a specialized format. Each message from your computer is a request to a server. You send a request, and they process it and return a response (data).

When you ask your computer to send a message to one of Google's servers, it first goes to a yellow-pages type address book where it looks up the IP address associated with "Google.com." This address book is called DNS (Domain Name System).

Now your browser has the IP address of the computer you want to message. Next, it sets up a TCP connection (we talked about this earlier) and begins sending and receiving messages.

**A quick summary before we move forward**

Computers talk to each other using some common protocols and languages. Different protocols are better suited for different kinds of communication. Each computer connected to the internet is like a house with its own unique IP address.

Since most humans can't remember thousands of IP addresses (at least I can't), they devised the concept of *domain names* and an automatic way of looking up someone's IP address if you just give them the domain. Computers send requests and responses back and forth in the form of data packets that travel through underground or underwater cables.

The messages are created and processed as per different protocols (TCP/IP, UDP, etc.), depending on the nature and purpose of the message.

**REST APIs**

You're already familiar with the concept of clients and servers from Chapter Three. A client can send different types of requests to a server:

1.   GET

2.   POST

3.   (+ 6 other less common types I won't mention, but you can look them up online)

GET and POST are usually analogous to read and write, respectively.

A GET (read-only) request simply asks for a certain piece of data and doesn't explicitly ask to change anything on the back-end, or in their database.

A POST request involves explicitly asking to change something on the back-end.

For example, when you enter Google.com on your browser, you're simply requesting to download the HTML and CSS code, etc. for Google's home page. You aren't asking Google to change or add data on their side.

But when you "like" something or submit a comment on Facebook, you send a POST request – you are asking to change something. While trying to log in to an email account online, you send a POST request – you are asking them to log you in and make a note of it in their database.

But it's not set in stone that you can only use GET requests for reads or POST requests for writes. The back-end engineer has complete control over which types of requests will be processed and how.

The whole concept of these request types is called "REST." What makes RESTful requests special is that they happen over the internet, often using the HTTP protocol.

This is why a lot of web APIs are "RESTful APIs" – they use requests defined by the HTTP protocol. It's an acronym that comes up a lot. Often you'll even come across RESTful microservices, which simply means that those microservices communicate with each other via REST APIs. This also makes them so much easier to externalize later on. (To understand why, you'll have to read Chapter Eight!)

———◆———

Chapter Five

# The Hidden Beauty of Databases

So far in the book, we've taken databases somewhat for granted. In most system diagrams, a database is depicted as a cylinder (as shown in the figure) that just sits there as an opaque black box, simply storing data.

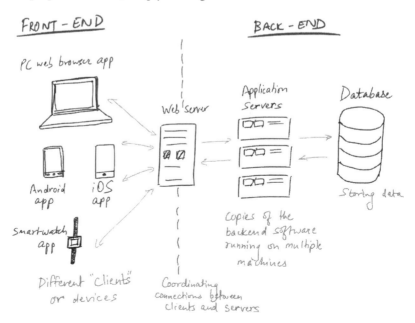

In reality – and you might laugh at me for saying this – modern database systems are so cool and sophisticated that I almost see them as living, breathing, constantly evolving digital creatures. They're the backbone of the digital world, and of your company too.

I can give it to you in writing that at least once in your business journey, you'll want to do something with your application such that an engineer will say, "well, the database isn't set up that way, but it's hard to explain why." A bad database setup is not only expensive to fix later but also a pain in the ass for whoever has to deal with it. So let's give databases the deep dive they deserve.

Now, this is the first of the "technical deep dive" chapters. This subject is quite large and complex (people do PhDs in databases), so I ask you to take it slow – don't just skim this chapter, and don't read it when you're tired or groggy. That being said, I've written it more like a story and not a textbook, so it shouldn't give you information overload!

First, we will build a software system for managing a traditional school library.

## Georgina Borrows A Book

Here's a use case: Georgina borrows a book. Let's follow the story.

Georgina enters the library, looks around, and picks up a book she likes (Shoe Dog). She goes to the lending desk, where Hiroko is working and says "I'd like to borrow this book!"

Hiroko asks Georgina if she has a membership card. She also needs to know if Georgina has any books overdue, if she has already borrowed her max number of books, etc.

Georgina says, "I don't have my card, but my phone number is 555-1234."

So here's our first set of requirements: The software shall have information about every library member. It shall allow us to search this data with multiple keys like phone number, membership number, etc. It shall also show a member's history of borrows and returns.

Say Georgina is all clear. Hiroko makes a new entry into the software that Georgina borrowed Shoe Dog.

The software shall have a catalog of all library books. It shall also allow making new entries that update a book's status and link it to a member.

Let's say the library's marketing team also has questions – they want to know which books are most popular, etc. So we also want to easily search the entire history of a book (who all have borrowed it and how long they kept it etc).

## The Classic Way

Personally, I grew up going to non-digital libraries. In case you did not have the same experience, here's a quick description of how they worked:

Each book had a little paper pocket glued inside the cover, with a small card inside it. When you borrowed a book, they'd remove this card, put the date and your name and ID on it, and keep it with them. They also had thick registers full of members' information. (I suspect they also had lists of all the books in the inventory but didn't keep it up-to-date.)

So at any given time, they had a stack of cards from all the books that had been borrowed. If you were late in returning the book, they could easily look up your phone/address from the register and send you a reminder. When you returned the book, they'd scratch out your name on the card and put it back in the paper pocket.

It's optimised for one objective – making sure that books get returned on time – and it's pretty effective at that. I loved the simplicity and elegance of this arrangement.

But let's say the library's marketing team came up with a question. (I only learned while writing this book that some libraries actually do have marketing teams. The more you know!) Consider this query: "Which were our five most popular books in the last year?"

In libraries that use the paper pocket system, this is a horribly difficult question to answer. It would take you several days (or maybe weeks) to search through the borrowing history of all the books.

To answer it quickly, you would have to organise the information in a totally different way – but that may have implications on how easy it is to track overdue books, etc. Or, you could make copies of the same data in different formats, to answer different types of queries.

Does that make conceptual sense? We'll come back to this later.

# Database Schemas

Coming back to the software, how would you organize all the raw data? Say you used simple spreadsheets. What different tables would you have to make, and with which columns?

These design details are called your "schema" (pronounced 'ski-ma').

Here's a possibility:

*Table 1: Members*

| NAME | MEMBER ID | PHONE | MEMBER SINCE | BOOKS LIMIT |
| --- | --- | --- | --- | --- |
| Georgina | 87651 | 555-1234 | Aug 11, 2019 | 3 |
| Abdul | 44320 | 656-1255 | March 07, 2017 | 3 |

*Table 2: Books*

| BOOK TITLE | BOOK ISBN | DATE ADDED | BOOK ID |
| --- | --- | --- | --- |
| Shoe Dog | ####87 | Jan 12, 2019 | AU-01 |
| Honoring the Self | ####09 | Oct 22, 2019 | NF-99 |
| Thinking Fast and Slow | ####11 | Apr 30, 2017 | EC-34 |

*Table 3: Transactions*

| MEMBER ID | BOOK ID | TYPE | DATE |
| --- | --- | --- | --- |
| 87651 | NF-99 | Borrow | June 1, 2020 |
| 87651 | EC-34 | Return | May 1, 2020 |
| 44320 | NF-99 | Return | April 25, 2020 |
| 87651 | EC-34 | Borrow | April 15, 2020 |

The Transactions table's entries link the previous two tables, *Members* and *Books*.

The above tables don't look beautiful so you may not have paid much attention to them (if I was in your place, I would have glossed over ugly tables with numbers too). But they're important and quite simple, so I won't let you get away easily! Let us follow the transaction in more detail:

**1. Searching for Georgina's information:** We look up the phone number in the Members table and see if the rest of the information (Name, etc) matches with the person.

| NAME | MEMBER ID | PHONE | MEMBER SINCE | BOOKS LIMIT |
|---|---|---|---|---|
| Georgina | 87651 | 555-1234 | Aug 11, 2019 | 3 |

We see that Georgina does exist in our database, and has a limit of borrowing up to 3 books at a time.

**2. Checking if Georgina has any overdue books**: Hmm, this seems tricky. Let's search the Transactions table with Georgina's member ID (87651). We see the following:

| MEMBER ID | BOOK ID | TYPE | DATE |
|---|---|---|---|
| 87651 (G) | NF-99 | Borrow | June 1, 2020 |
| 87651 (G) | EC-34 | Return | May 1, 2020 |
| 87651 (G) | EC-34 | Borrow | April 15, 2020 |

Notice that this table acts as a 'link' between Members and Books.

So it seems like we have 3 entries: Georgina borrowed and returned a book previously, and currently has one book (NF-99, or *Steal Like An Artist*) that she hasn't returned.

Now, we need to decide if that book is overdue or not. You may not have realized this, but our schema doesn't yet include a way of telling this!

- Should we have an extra column in the Books table, saying how long each book can be borrowed?

- Or should this apply to Members instead (different members can borrow books for different durations depending on how much they paid, perhaps)?

- Should it simply be a fixed duration for all books and all members, removing the immediate need for storing it in the database?

These are highly contextual non-technical / business decisions, but they directly influence how the database schema would be designed.

It's quite hard to change the database schema once it has been set up, so it should be done with care. It's not unusual for people to be forced to recreate a database from scratch and spend a few days copying and reproducing all the data.

Moreover, notice that I kept the Transactions separate from the *Members* and *Books* tables. When someone borrows or returns a book, I don't want to add that information into a new column or row in the *Members* or *Books* tables. Keeping information separate allows us to keep things clean! This is an example of a best practice. Engineers have many best practices for designing database schemas so they are less likely to have issues.

**3. Making new entries, and asking complex questions:** When we let her borrow Shoe Dog, we make one more entry to the Transactions table. Later, when she comes back and returns it, we'd add another entry to the same table. This way, we can store much better records about the Library's operations. It also enables us to answer more intelligent questions such as:

- "Which are our 5 most popular books? We may want to order more copies." -> Simply go through the transactions table and count which book IDs appear the most often.

- "Who are our 10 most active members from the last month? We want to send a gift." -> Look at which member IDs appeared the most often in the transactions table.

- "Of all the members that have ever borrowed Shoe Dog, how many of them have been members for at least a year?" -> You would have to cross-relate data from all three tables, but it's not too complicated.

Just by changing the way information is stored, these queries went from being notoriously difficult to answer, to being very easy and straightforward!

You can probably see that there is no right or wrong answer for how to design the best schema for a particular database. The schema depends on the goals of the organization. A bank, a hospital, a library, etc all have very different data needs and have to answer different types of queries on a daily basis, so the schemas are unique.

In finance and accounting, everybody uses double-entry bookkeeping. It is a format for recording transactions and involves having two columns in a ledger instead of a single column. Unless you've dabbled in finance, this may not seem like a very powerful example to you. But without this two-column schema, even simple queries like calculating monthly profit and loss is a tedious and tiresome task. Double-entry ledgers were independently invented in different places throughout history, but really exploded in popularity in the 1400s, when an Italian monk wrote a book on the subject and turned accounting into a science. A simple change in how you record transactions made doing business so easy, that it helped propel our world into the golden age of modern finance – one we're still living in.

I find that fascinating. By the way, did you know that the oldest surviving records of humans doing math, by making inscriptions on clay tablets and bones, are all related to accounting? Our ancestors only cared about abstract concepts like adding and subtracting numbers as long as it helped them figure out how much money they're owed by their neighbor. (I do wonder how modern imaginary numbers like $\sqrt{-1}$ would have been received in those days.)

**Quick recap:**

- You have two basic types of operations with data: *reads* and *writes*.

- Depending on the application, you decide:

    1. What *types* of information you need to store in the database

    2. The kinds of *queries* that would be performed against that data

- Based on the above, you decide your database *schema*. Even though there are no right/wrong answers, there are always best practices you can follow while developing a new schema for a given purpose.

# Relational/SQL Databases

What you saw above is called a relational database (RDB). Its schema has tables with rows and columns. Each entity (Member, Book, Transaction, etc) has its own separate table.

Then you have commands to select, insert, update or delete data. All these are different types of queries. Because these relational databases have a strict, *structured* schema chosen carefully at the beginning, they need you to use a *structured query language*

(SQL) to look up information. You can manipulate thousands (if not millions) of rows of data with a single line of SQL code. SQL is scary – if you make a big mistake that updates thousands of rows, there is no simple way of undoing a change to a database. But, for the same reasons, it is also a very powerful language.

In fact, SQL is so popular that relational databases are also referred to as SQL databases! They store all the information in tables with fixed columns, which can run into billions of rows. In SQL databases, the data is more consistent and reliable. This makes it easier to read (or look up) information. A lot of financial organizations use SQL databases at the core. Having strict schemas lets them be more careful about what they are writing to their database (adding new entries or modifying/deleting existing ones), and helps keep the integrity of the data.

But like most other things in this world, nothing is perfect. There are also some problems with SQL databases, which we'll discuss next.

## Challenges With Relational Databases

### Changing Schemas

Imagine if the library wanted to add a new program – *a special membership for children.*

Let's say they want to introduce these controls:

1.  Classify books as kid-friendly or not (= adding a "kid-friendly" column to the *Books* table)

2.  Store members' birthdays, to discern their age (= adding a "birth date" column to *Members*)

3.  Update the application with new features, such as allowing kids to borrow more books than the regular limit. Or, letting them keep books for longer.

The original application is already live, and the database is constantly in use every day. Making these changes would mean taking it offline, updating the schema, updating the data carefully, updating all the application code that depends on that schema, and making it live again.

Personally, I wouldn't make a change like this. Remember what we discussed in the last chapter, about good testing culture and phase-by-phase deployment? The ideal way would be to build a completely separate prototype application for the kid-based features, to test the idea and make quick modifications based on feedback before integrating it with the main application.

For some big and more sensitive systems, it can be prohibitively expensive to make changes to the schema on the fly. Engineers might fight you over it, and for good reason.

So as the first obvious downside, once SQL databases grow in size, it's not simple to change the schema into whatever you like.

## Scaling Reliably

Usually, when you can't fit all your personal data into a single hard disk, what do you do? The first option is to get a bigger hard disk. This is called vertical scaling. Of course, vertical scaling has limits – after a while, buying a bigger disk gets too expensive to be practical. The other option is to split your data and store it in multiple smaller hard disks. This is called horizontal scaling. In database terms, it's also called "sharding" the data.

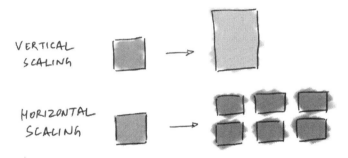

What challenges can you imagine with sharding a database?

The general sentiment is that we all want our data to be "reliable." In the world of databases, this fuzzy universal notion of reliability has a more precise definition. SQL databases are designed to always have four properties, called ACID properties:

1.  Atomicity: Either all the operations of a transaction reflect in the database or none.

2.  Consistency: Data across the entire database should be consistent; no errors.

3.  Isolation: One transaction should start execution only when the other finishes execution.

4.   Durability: Changes made into the database should be permanent even if there is a system failure. You should be able to dig out a dead database machine from under the rocks and still access all its data.

All these rules are great. But they also act as constraints and sacrifice some speed and flexibility.

When you have many different tables, and each of them is connected to each other (eg. the *Transactions* table refers to both Members and Books), you still have to keep those connections intact when you split and move the data to separate machines. As the amount of data scales up to millions and billions of rows across hundreds of tables (not uncommon for social media and banking/financial databases), this gets computationally harder to do.

Next, what if one of the machines got damaged, and you suddenly lost a large piece of data that was supposed to be connected to other data, thus potentially corrupting the entire database across all the machines. For this reason, you also want copies of every single sharded machine, as a back-up. These back-up copies also help reduce the *load* on the database. When you have a huge number of concurrent queries coming to the database, splitting them across multiple machines is helpful.

But making copies opens another can of worms. You have to keep them up to date and consistent! Every change you make on one machine, has to be replicated on its backup machine. When you have a lot of different machines with different pieces of data, keeping them consistent 100% of the time can hurt performance.

So what's an elegant solution to this problem? If you think about it, "consistency" doesn't have to be black or white. It's a continuum, with many shades of gray.

*Strong consistency* would mean that as soon as a single change is made anywhere in the database, you make sure it's reflected across every copy of that data before you make any more changes. *Weak consistency* might look like this: you allow different shards or copies to be inconsistent, and then update them only once in a while.

Between these two extremes, there's a lot of space for *eventual consistency*. How consistent does your database need to be? That depends on your application and product roadmap.

The tech community has worked to fix the above problems for a long time, so you don't have to reinvent the wheel. Today, most databases are offered as a service that packs solutions to all the above issues. They can handle much of the scaling automatically and also enable eventual consistency – though it runs into limits the bigger you get.

Therefore, you'll often hear about a *database server* (just like an application server) that gives you database access through an API. There are many such SQL databases on the market, available both commercially and open source, such as MySQL (famously used by Facebook), Postgres (used by Instagram), etc. You don't have to remember these names, so just know that they all operate a little bit differently in terms of scaling, handling concurrent requests, etc.

Take a short break and reflect on what you just learned.

## "Not only SQL"

There are some things that you just can't do within the confines of tables and rows. So it comes as no surprise that the industry has developed alternatives.

Take a look at the dictionary page in the figure.

| amputate | 22 | ancient |
|---|---|---|

am·pli·fy (am'plə fī') ◻verb amplified, amplifying, amplifies
amputate verb To cut off part of: *amputated a finger.*
am·pu·tate (am'pyoo tāt') ◻verb amputated, amputating, amputates
amuse verb 1. To hold someone's attention in a pleasant or agreeable way: *She amused us with adventure stories.* 2. To cause to laugh or smile: *The new toy amused the child.*
a·muse (ə myōōz') ◻verb amused, amusing, amuses

SYNONYMS: amuse, divert, entertain
These verbs mean to hold someone's attention in a pleasant or agreeable way: *The visit to the zoo*

analysis noun The separation of something into its basic parts to find out what it contains or is made of: *An analysis of the water showed that it contained chemical pollutants.*
a·nal·y·sis (ə nal'i sis) ◻noun, plural a·nal·y·ses (ə nal'i sēz')
analyze verb 1. To separate something into its basic parts to find out what it contains or is made of: *They analyzed the ore and found iron in it.* 2. To examine in detail: *We analyzed our plan to see why it had failed.*
an·a·lyze (an'ə līz') ◻verb analyzed, analyzing, analyzes
anatomy noun 1. The scientific study of the structure of animals and plants. 2. The structure of an animal or plant: *We studied the anatomy of the butterfly in science class*

For the word "amputate," the entry has one definition, then an example, then its phonetic pronunciation, and then 3 verb forms (amputated, amputating, amputates). But for the word "amuse," the entry includes two definitions, with one example each. And for "anatomy," there are two definitions but only one example!

Now imagine if you wanted to convert this dictionary into a spreadsheet table. Due to all the variations, it would be one ugly spreadsheet with uneven numbers of columns.

This is an example of a data structure where the relational way of storing data, with all its rows and columns, is not only unnecessary but would make your life harder.

The most popular kind of non-relational data structure is a dictionary, as you saw in the above example. Here, the *key* is the word you want to look up, and the value is the dictionary entry for that word. There's also an *ordering* mechanism that helps you find the key very easily (alphabetical order etc). Therefore, most NoSQL databases are actually just "key-value stores." It's a very common and elegant way of storing data. Each dictionary entry also acts as a mini-document, so you'll also often hear them being called "document-oriented databases."

Can you see how it would be much easier to add extra information to a flexible document versus a rigid table? This is why such databases can often handle a lot of write requests in parallel. They're widely used for *write-heavy* workloads. A lack of consistency is very convenient when you care about writing as much data as possible, as quickly as possible.

Most companies use *both* SQL and NoSQL databases, and copy data from one to the other depending on how they want to use it. They keep a combination of structured and unstructured data. Many people like sticking to a rule of thumb: *use SQL for read-heavy workloads, and NoSQL for write-heavy.* There are other kinds of data stores which aren't even considered databases at all, such as "event logs," but they're beyond the scope of this book.

Here's a simple analogy: the less rigid a data structure is (eg: a blank canvas), the more freedom you have in writing to it, thus making it "write-heavy."

A great use case for write-heavy data storage is app analytics. When you use YouTube or Facebook, in the background, they're collecting as much data from your activity as possible. From tracking your scrolling behavior, to whose pictures you're looking at for how long, and even details like the messages you write but decide to delete before you send them – all this information is going back to their data stores, in parallel from billions of people's accounts.

If you're building an application where your customers' activity data will be very important, and having new ideas each week for what kind of data you could collect from user accounts, you don't want to update an SQL database schema each time. So it might make sense to use a flexible datastore.

Or, if you were building a digital currency for your country and wanted to be able to monitor the flow of money, you might choose to store the core transaction data in a SQL database – each transaction record would have information like sender ID, recipient ID, amount of money, time of transaction, etc. But you may also keep a mirror or copy of this database in a NoSQL database – this way, if you decide to capture more types of information, you could simply put the new data into your NoSQL mirror database. No need to change the SQL schema.

Anyway, depending on the situation, you can always plug and play different technologies. Today's data systems are sophisticated engineering marvels in their own right, and are still evolving.

But hey — don't stress your brain trying to memorize all this. All we care about building is intuition, which I hope you've been able to develop through this chapter.

———◆———

You've reached the half-way point of this book! I'm glad you're enjoying it.

Quick request. You know better than anyone what it's like to be in *your* situation and which challenges you're trying to overcome. And there's probably someone else out there in your shoes, who is looking at this book online and is on the fence trying to make a judgment about whether it's worth reading it. They're reading other people's reviews, but what they really want is an opinion of someone *similar to themselves.*

If understand you may be pressed for time. But if you'd like to help them make this decision, please leave an honest **review** on this book's page on Amazon, or wherever else you got it, or even your social media/blog. As you write the review, please share a little about your particular situation (why you got the book) and the advice you'd give to someone else like you. Thanks!

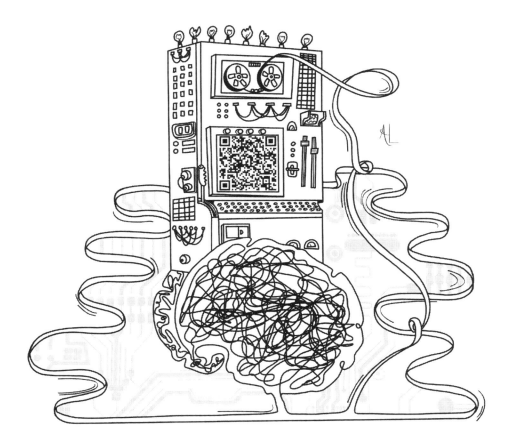

**Artist: Alena (Gonzales) Lundberg (USA)**

*Scan this artwork like a QR code for optional bonus content.*

Chapter Six

# Building for Billions

In 1886, a wounded American Civil War soldier, who was addicted to morphine, developed a flavored non-alcoholic drink that contained cocaine and caffeine as supposedly healthier substitutes for the problematic drug. Soon, he started selling it out of a small pharmacy in Atlanta, Georgia for five cents per glass, advertising it as a "wonder medicine" that helped with everything from morphine addiction to headaches and male impotence.

This cocaine cocktail became spectacularly popular (surprise surprise), so in order to grow sales beyond his little corner of the street, he shifted to a franchising model for production and distribution. He would keep the recipe secret, and sell only the concentrated syrup to other pharmacies. They would then dilute the syrup with water and sell the final product out of a soda machine.

It worked, and the drink soon went from "medicine" to a mainstream beverage. That's when they stopped dealing with pharmacies and turned their ambitions toward large bottling plants.

Today, Coca-Cola has franchise bottlers all over the planet, as the world's biggest beverage company. They still sell concentrated syrup to franchisees and it accounts for most of their revenue, although the secret recipe no longer contains cocaine.

In the early 2000s, they experimented with skipping franchisees and owning their own bottling plants – to have full control over their quality and growth in certain markets. But after some time, they realized that having so many more delivery trucks, warehouses and a bunch of other assets was an expensive overhead, so they soon returned to their roots in franchising.

The company still completely owns the brand and does its own marketing and advertising to promote the product. But when you buy a bottle or can, it's sold by a franchisee, not by the Coca-Cola company.

Now, consider another crazy possibility – why doesn't Coca-Cola sell their concentrated syrup to consumers like you and me directly? Why can't we buy little pouches and sachets of coke syrup that you can mix in your kitchen?

Well for one, it could be that most people don't have a soda machine to put the fizz into bottles. But more importantly, the ultimate reason is simply *that Coca-Cola chose to do it this way.* They chose their business model. That's really it!

Herein we see a simple, fundamental truth about scaling a business – it's very subjective. Depending on the nature of the product and the business, there are different ways to scale. A large factory is not simply a bigger version of a small one. The infrastructure can be fundamentally different, whether it's the tools and techniques, or the specializations of the staff involved.

Two Rolex watches sold anywhere in the world come from a single factory in Geneva, Switzerland. Ferrari cars are also made in a single factory in Italy – founded in 1939, they kept moving from smaller to bigger factories over the years.

The same applies to software systems, and that is the focus of this chapter. There are many ways to go about creating software architecture and infrastructure that can scale, and you should choose the one that compliments your business strategy the most.

We already touched on scaling databases in the last chapter. Now, it's time to look at all the different aspects of scalability – architecture, design, infrastructure, etc. – from a more comprehensive point of view. You'll also hear some fun stories about how to build applications that deal with hundreds of millions of people (or dollars, traffic, whatever):

- Netflix (single-handedly accounts for 10-20% of worldwide internet traffic with over 200 million customers)

- Dropbox (700+ million accounts with over 550 billion pieces of content)

- Plenty of Fish (an online dating website that scaled to over 6 billion page views per month with a *single employee*)

By the way, it goes without saying that scaling the software infrastructure of a *product* is just half the battle. Scaling is also an internal problem — how do you manage thousands of engineers without reverting to chaos or becoming a slow bureaucratic monster? That is an operations problem, which deserves its own book, but we will look at some aspects of it in Chapter Nine.

Let's go!

## Splitting the Load

The core concept of scalability is simple and straightforward: *doing more*. When scaling anything (whether a hospital ward or a web application), it usually means the following:

1. Handling more requests (throughput)

2. Managing more assets (capacity)

There are two ways you can go about it:

1. Vertical scaling: if what you have isn't good enough, get something bigger or faster

2. Horizontal scaling: replicate the resource and split the load between them

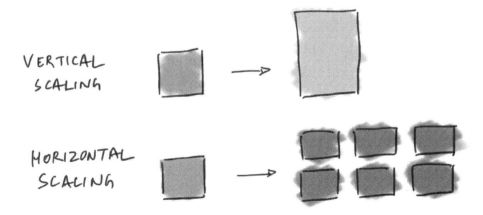

Scaling horizontally is attractive because it's usually cheaper and faster than having to move things altogether from one machine to another. It's also much more flexible, and makes it easier to scale back down! For example, if some servers have a problem or are no longer needed, you can easily remove or replace them. The same issue in a single large server could cause an outage.

Here's a fun fact: in 2010, the US Air Force connected 1,760 Playstation gaming consoles to create a supercomputer. Yes, you read that right. They used this cluster to quickly process satellite images and other things, and it was the fastest computer in the entire US Defense Department. Second-hand Playstations used to be quite popular among scientists who couldn't afford expensive computers.

On the downside, as we saw with sharded databases, orchestrating the operations of many machines at the same time is a headache. The more you scale, the more custom software it takes just to monitor and manage all those servers, and keep everything functional. These software costs can add up. Companies like Google and Facebook, which have *millions* of servers, not only have to build huge data centers, but also hire thousands of world-class engineers to run them.

A rack of servers at a data center – each server has its own CPU and memory

On the other hand, in 2008, a Canadian dating website called Plenty of Fish, run by a single person (its founder), accomplished 1.2 billion page views per month using *vertical scaling*. Instead of having thousands of small servers, they scaled up by only buying two monstrously powerful servers. The high-end hardware easily cost them upwards of $100,000, but saved a lot more in software and power costs (it takes much more energy to run 1,000 small computers than two large ones).

There's no clear-cut barrier or pros & cons list between vertical and horizontal scaling – it's usually a hybrid. In Chapter Eight, you'll learn to see which individual part of the system you're trying to scale and be better able to estimate the costs of scaling it up or out.

All this – both the hardware and software – is part of your company's *IT Infrastructure*. Many tech companies have engineering departments with dozens (or even hundreds) of people solely dedicated to infrastructure.

## Load Balancing

When you scale horizontally (multiple facilities sharing the load), every time you get a new request, how do you choose which facility will take care of it?

You could decide to keep one facility working extremely busy throughout the day, with the other facility acting as a reserve resource. During periods of peak load, you could send the "overflowing" requests to the reserve facility. Or, you might want to keep all your facilities equally busy all the time, so that none is ever under too much strain.

How do you keep them equally busy? You could send requests to each facility one by one in a fixed order, or have a fancier algorithm that monitors every facility's load, and sends each new request to the least busy one.

Whichever way you choose to distribute or "balance" the load between multiple facilities, the fact remains that you have to do it somehow.

This is called *load balancing*, and it is a critical concept in scaling software. You have to manage and regulate how busy each server will be. A load balancer is a little machine or piece of software that does exactly that – when the back-end receives a new request, the load balancer is the first thing the request interacts with – it selects which server will respond to that request, and sends it there.

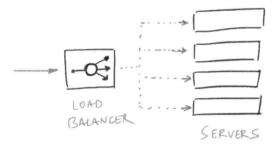

I'm glad that its name is very straightforward, so you'll never have to memorize it.

## Caching (pronounced *"cash-ing"*)

A cache is another cornerstone of scalability, without which, much of the world's databases would be falling apart from the load. If you've ever found yourself deleting questionable internet history in your web browser, you may have seen an option called "clear cache."

To explain what it is, I'll use an analogy. Let's say you worked in the box office/ front booth of a cinema theater. Customers come to you to ask for information, or for ticketing.

If you have 200 people waiting outside and 80% of them just keep asking you for basic information, it's a terrible use of your time. You want to focus on ticket bookings and more special queries.

A great way to reduce the number of queries would be to put a table/chart outside that shows exactly all the shows scheduled for the next 3 days, along with other common information. Most people can now just see the chart and walk away without getting in line. Due to the time saved, both general user queries and new ticket booking requests can get served much quicker.

These tables and charts are optimized for reads and not writes (most people will just look up information, not add to the chart). That's okay; it only needs to be written when there's a change.

The chart on the wall is our *cache.*

Storing commonly requested data in a read-optimized cache (especially for a public-facing portal) greatly reduces the load on your DB. This increases the speed at which *both read and write requests* can get served.

Your browser has a cache too – often images take more time to load on the first time, but if you refresh the page it's much quicker. This is because the image got stored in the cache, and doesn't need to be fetched from the back-end again and again.

While reloading the page, your browser first checks if it's in the cache (like the cinema booth customer), and if not, *then* it makes a request to the back-end.

The bigger and more sophisticated your cache is, the fewer requests your DB has to handle. The only "cost" of the cache is the space it takes up on the wall (storage space or RAM), and the time/energy cost of keeping it up to date.

Of course, if your cinema is located in a little village of 100 people in the middle of nowhere and only five show up to your box in a day, you don't need a cache. Caching is more valuable when you're getting to scale, or when each DB operation is so complex that you'd like to filter DB requests from day one.

Today, with many public-facing websites (such as Reddit), the cache is often a **key-value store** that can be bigger than DB itself – because after all, storage space is quite cheap in the 21st century. They can even have multiple clones of the data relevant to each user, in the cache. This way, the server only queries the database when you change *(=write)* something. For all other operations, it reads from the cache, which is always updated as soon as the database is.

In essence, you can use a non-relational datastore to scale a relational database more easily!

## CDNs

If you log into your Netflix account from outside the USA, say Korea, and watch a popular show like Our Planet, chances are that the content would not be streamed from their servers in the USA, but from a location within Korea. The reason is simple and fairly obvious: any lag or buffer time can worsen the viewing experience, so they want to transmit the video data to you from a shorter distance.

This is done using a *Content Delivery Network* (CDN). Using a CDN means that most of your heavy assets (images, video, audio, etc), instead of being stored on a central datastore are copied and distributed separately, "hosted" in many locations around the world.

CDNs also offer other built-in features which make the distribution of content easier. One of them is storing different versions of the same file, optimized for diverse devices and internet speeds: for example, they'll send a low-resolution image to someone with bad internet, instead of making them wait a long time to fully load the page. Most companies pay a service provider to maintain the global network, but the big tech giants like Facebook have their own.

Take a very short break to review what you've learned.

# The Curious Case of Cloud Computing

A lot of people believe that a company should only focus on doing things that differentiate them from their competition and build a better relationship with customers – *the core competencies* – and everything else should be delegated or outsourced.

Therefore, a lot of companies completely outsource their IT operations headaches to someone else and focus on building products for customers and running a business instead.

This gave rise to the *cloud computing* industry, where companies offer remote servers and scalability as a service. All you have to do is build your product/app and give it to them. They'll put it on their own servers and scale automatically as the load increases.

As of 2022, the biggest cloud services providers are Amazon Web Services (AWS), Microsoft Azure, Google Cloud, and IBM. There's also Alibaba Cloud and Tencent Cloud in China.

Recently, it's been very popular for companies to *migrate to the cloud* – shutting down their data centers and outsourcing everything.

Let's look at some case studies.

The first one is Netflix, which started outsourcing its I.T. in 2008 and unplugged its last data center in 2016, and should probably be sponsoring me for mentioning them a hundred times in this book. After moving everything to the cloud, they now focus only on their *product* – the movie library, recommendations, and streaming technology. It's estimated that they pay out more than US$100M to their cloud computing partners (mainly Amazon).

Then there's Uber – in the early days, they were growing so fast that their *highest* amount of server traffic in a given month would be their average traffic in the next month. They too adopted cloud computing (from both Google and Amazon), because it allowed them to automatically handle spikes in traffic such as during the holiday season. Their competitor Lyft also solely uses cloud computing. Between 2019 and 2021, Lyft had a contract to pay at least US$300 million to Amazon for their cloud. Companies on a hypergrowth trajectory should stick to the cloud.

Dropbox, on the other hand, took a different approach. They started out using Amazon (as a hypergrowth company), but once they got to a certain scale, they realized that as a data storage company, they had special performance needs that Amazon couldn't satisfy. So they did something that was almost unheard of: in 2015, seven years after founding, they began moving away from the cloud and onto their own data centers! Based on their calculations, engineering their own data hardware from scratch would give them a significant competitive advantage and price savings. Looking back, they believe it was the right decision.

The lesson here is that cloud computing services are awesome, and they may not be for everyone, but they're *probably* right for you. They make it easy to launch your application, have low upfront costs, and save you plenty of time.

## Key Takeaway

From a business standpoint, the cornerstone of scalability is marginal cost. That is, reducing the extra resources (raw materials, energy, and time) that you need to do a certain thing one more time.

Adding one more passenger to a two-hour flight on an Airbus A320 only costs the airline around 10 additional gallons of gas that the plane would burn to carry the extra weight, the packet of peanuts, and no extra time. At some point, there would come a saturation point (such as when the plane is full) and the marginal cost would include shifting to bigger *infrastructure*, i.e. moving all passengers and goods to a bigger plane or multiple smaller planes.

The same applies to digital companies. There are plenty of service providers out there, as well as geeks within your company, who may want you to invest in prematurely scaling your back-end because "why not." In fact, this is such a growing problem that unsurprisingly, another new breed of consultants has risen in recent years to do "FinOps" – they help companies reduce their cloud computing bills.

So, how do you avoid getting lost in the best practices, and figure out what kind of infrastructure you need to go from A to B, and then from C to G, based on your needs? As we discussed in Chapter Four with the FBI story, the answer involves having a sound technical architecture or blueprint which can guide all those decisions. It's a mix of art, science and common sense. We will dive deep into architecture and system design in Chapter Eight, so keep reading!

**Artist: Gihantha Gunasekara (Sri Lanka)**

*Scan this artwork like a QR code for optional bonus content.*

Chapter Seven

# Keep Your Naughty Hat On

In 2000, a 15-year-old boy in Montréal, Canada, ran a software program on his personal computer that attacked and shut down Yahoo.com, the world's top internet company and search engine at the time, for a whole hour — just for fun. Encouraged by the results, he then proceeded to bring down Amazon, eBay, CNN, and several other big sites within the next week.

It was estimated that he had single-handedly caused damages of over US$1.5 billion. More importantly, he had sent a clear message to the world: if the world's largest websites can be rendered inaccessible by a school kid, then most government and corporate IT systems were effectively defenseless. It inspired a whole generation of "hackers" and launched a new gold rush of cyber-crime. Even U.S. President Bill Clinton was alarmed and got involved.

While the boy, Michael Calce, was prosecuted and sent to jail as a teenager, the CIA still credits him for their greatly increased investments into online security over the next decade.

There was a time when it didn't matter if you were Google, Facebook, Mastercard, or even Burger King — everyone got cyber-attacked eventually. Today, it still doesn't matter who you are, but the difference is that now you get attacked every single day, and some of the attacks are *successful* eventually.

That brings us to this chapter. As a modern executive, your journey of technical fluency is severely incomplete without a discussion of cybersecurity. You may have been told about "best practices" if you've ever had to participate in corporate training, such as "don't open suspicious emails," "use a password manager," etc. Instead, we'll look under the hood and understand how it *really* works — the psychology, economics, and tactics of cyber-warfare.

Let me show you around.

## What does it mean to be "hacked"?

Let's do a mischievous thought experiment.

Say you want to do something *bad* to a restaurant. Remember that whatever you do, it would cost you time, effort, and maybe money, so you want to profit from this operation if possible.

Naturally, the first question is *what should you do?* It depends on your goals. Examples:

- Infiltrate the kitchen and spoil ingredients, damage the equipment, etc.

- Steal their secret recipes.

- Plot with someone to steal money from their cash registers.

- Impersonate a customer and steal the pre-paid food delivery.

- Hire people to crowd the restaurant before peak hour and waste their time, so that their target customers can't get any service.

- Shut down their power abruptly during peak service hours.

- Intercept a food delivery and switch the food with candied chicken.

(It's just a coincidence that these seem to get progressively worse.)

It's not possible to do anything you want, so you may also first need to do a *recon mission* — going and poking around the restaurant to look for vulnerabilities. For example, when they're receiving new supplies, is there a small window of time when nobody's paying attention and you could sneak in through the back? Are their door locks new or old, and which kind? Etc etc. The vulnerabilities you find will often dictate which crimes you can pull off, as well as the game plan for achieving your nefarious goals.

But you get the idea — any part of the system can be attacked. Unsurprisingly, you can apply the same creativity to software systems.

You could have a Denial of Service or "DoS" attack (=crowding the restaurant), "Man in the Middle" (=eavesdropping), Phishing (=impersonation), Malware (=spoiling someone's kitchen), Ransomware (=stealing data and holding it ransom), etc.

The whole field of cybersecurity is about reducing the risk of each of these. Depending on the nature of your business or application, some of these attacks would be much more damaging than others.

## The Target "Heist"

In 2013, the American retailer Target fell victim to a cyber attack. The hackers stole the personal data of 70 million customers, including 40 million credit and debit cards. Target got drowned in lawsuits, lost hundreds of millions of dollars, and its CEO had to resign after he had been working there since 1979. Let this sink in for a moment.

The hack itself was quite interesting. Just like in the typical heist movie, the attackers did something similar to impersonating a supplier and using their ID to sneak into the building. Once inside, they'd do more tinkering experiments, cracking one lock after another until they could penetrate the vault full of gold.

First, the hackers sent a *phishing* email to one of Target's refrigeration contractors. They pretended to send a harmless link or attachment, which when opened, managed to trick one of their employees into downloading a virus onto their computer. (Most modern data breaches start with phishing; the most infamous was Yahoo! compromising **three billion** user accounts in 2013.) Using this computer virus, the hackers stole the employee's login password for Target's *vendor portal*.

Once inside, they started doing lots of *reconnaissance*. They poked around for security vulnerabilities to sneak into Target's IT systems (there are techniques for doing so, like "database injection" but I won't explain right now what that means).

The hackers followed this process for longer, continually doing reconnaissance and breaking into one piece of the system after another until they reached the core of the company's operations, including where they hold credit card information.

Finally, the hackers needed to make changes at the *administrator level* but had to first ask for authorization. When they tried to use a fake/stolen identity to make the request, it raised a red flag in their system. But it seems that nobody took it seriously, and the result is for all of us to see.

That's what we mean by "hacking." It's not like in the movies where someone types on their keyboard for a few seconds and "hacks into the mainframe" (gosh I hate that line), instantly taking control of an entire system and making it do whatever they want. Even for a simple system, it's **surprisingly hard** to pull off, if not impossible, unless the person who built it is a complete dummy.

## Let's talk defense

Again we'll start with the restaurant. How would you safeguard yourself against the different kinds of attacks?

- Watch out for any strangers snooping around. Prevent reconnaissance. Invest in surveillance, such as CCTV cameras, and burglar alarms.

- Have a culture of bringing attention to any occurrence that's unfamiliar or out of the ordinary — if something has no explanation, people should care enough to investigate it.

- Don't authorize everyone to access everything (Does the sous-chef really need a key to your cash register?)

- Have backups for things that would drive you out of business if they broke down (like the power generator).

- Regularly check all ingredients and dishes for taste/contamination/spoilage, and keep all surfaces clean.

- Secure all doors and windows. Change the locks unpredictably.

- Have a "decoy" cash register that contains Monopoly money, while the real cash is hidden away (!)

If you know your business well, you can imagine the most destructive ways it could be attacked, and thus devise a series of processes to prevent that from happening. Often, you may even sacrifice one type of security for another.

Let's put this in the context of the Target Hack.

Remember how it started when they stole a password to the vendor portal? There lies the first thing that could have made this attack harder: requiring *two-factor authentication* to log in to any of Target's portals. (Two-factor means they don't just let you sign in with a password, but also send a one-time code to your phone to confirm.)

The hackers' next step was reconnaissance, which creates the second opportunity for defense: Whenever people are actively poking around your system for vulnerabilities, their behavior is very abnormal and suspicious compared to the average user who's just trying to get their work done. Digitally, this is even more apparent because you can analyze the record of all the things a person is trying to do. If Target had been monitoring even the most basic user activity (to see if nothing's suspicious), it could have been detected.

Then, it's interesting that the attackers could start with a simple vendor portal, and then find a path to more and more sensitive parts of the system! When every piece of a system is closely interlinked to each other, the whole system can become vulnerable if one component gets compromised. The most sensitive pieces should ideally be isolated from the rest of the system and put under extra security.

That being said, this has both pros and cons. On the flip side, the more you separate the parts of a software system and spread them over distances, the more things can individually go wrong, and the more things you have to keep track of! There are always trade-offs that engineers work with. (It all begins with the technical architecture — which we'll discuss in the next chapter.)

Finally, the hackers had to ask for authorization to get administrator privileges, setting off an alarm, it should have been the ultimate foil. If anyone had investigated the warning or if the process had stricter two-factor verification, it might have been prevented.

There's no such thing as a foolproof system. I'm not trying to crucify Target engineers here, and you can see that hacking Target wasn't a walk in the park. The attackers only persisted this far because the payoffs were huge — tens of millions of credit cards!

As a general rule, most hackers are after money. They're either looking to steal data that they can sell on the black market, ask you for a ransom, or ask your customers for a ransom. (My sister, a cybersecurity enthusiast, once found my email password for sale online. It was a fun day. For her.) Correspondingly, the way to deter them is to make the hack more and more expensive, thus thinning their profit margins. That's what central banks do to prevent counterfeit paper currency — they simply make the banknotes more expensive to forge.

A solid defense strategy begins with understanding what's most valuable if lost, then wondering about ways it could be attacked, and putting the respective safeguards and monitoring in place.

This brings me to another fun fact — computers that controlled US nuclear missiles were, even until 2019, not connected to the internet, and used good old 8-inch floppy disks for sharing information since the '70s. Fairly un-hackable unless you pulled off a Mission Impossible and physically infiltrated heavily guarded facilities.

There are also state-funded hackers who don't care about profits — they're given a mission and must grind till it's over, and have ample resources to go the extra mile. In 2014, a cyber army allegedly from North Korea broke into Sony Pictures' data and demanded that they cancel the release of their then-upcoming comedy film, *The Interview* — which featured an assassination attempt on Kim Jong-un. If you, gentle reader, are ever on the receiving end of a state-sponsored cyber attack, I first offer you my condolences, as well as congratulations on not living a boring life. The specific strategies for dealing with this are outside the scope of this book, but the cyber security principles remain the same.

That being said, I can't leave you empty-handed, so let's discuss one popular kind of cyber-attack that state-funded operations like to use.

## Denial of Service

As we discussed before, a "denial of service" type of attack on your servers is like crowding a restaurant with fake customers so that their real customers can't get service.

In a DoS attack, your back-end infrastructure receives a sudden spike in requests, without warning. As we saw in the previous chapter, if your system is not meant to handle that kind of scale, it will break down and your software will become unusable.

It's not meant to generate a profit; its only purpose is to overwhelm and block you from operating altogether. It is also much cheaper and more straightforward to overpower someone's systems with sheer traffic than to plan an elaborate secret heist, thus making it a very sinister and effective tool.

This is the exact same type of attack that 15-year-old Michael Calce, mentioned in the opening story of this chapter, deployed to bring down big websites.

Here are two simple and intuitive ideas for how to defend against DoS.

1. You could choose to always keep some extra spare capacity. If there's a sudden flood of customers, the buffer would buy you time to react before you get overwhelmed.

2. One tactic is to reduce the *rate* at which you receive each request. This is like having a long waiting line outside your store. You hold all traffic at the load balancer's level and limit the speed at which the requests enter and reach your app servers. You don't distinguish between good or bad traffic, so even real customer requests are held off. It's slow and frustrating, and some customers will leave, but it's better than having chaos inside the store.

Both of these are fairly standard ways to protect your back-end servers from getting damaged. However, building a buffer isn't a defense. Moreover, reducing the rate of requests indiscriminately no matter where they come from would mean your real customers get slower service, potentially making them upset. With either defense, the attacker effectively succeeds!

What we need is a way to *distinguish* the bad traffic and keep it out, while letting in the good traffic. For example, if you notice that a huge traffic spike is coming from 4 tiny islands in the Pacific, or if all of those requests share certain keywords, you can be pretty sure it's a hacker trying to DoS you. So you could immediately block *all traffic* from those sources until the attack dies down.

Moreover, in the last chapter, you also learned about tools like caching, CDNs, and load balancing. Not only are they helpful to handle *scale,* but they can also act as a protective layer around your servers and databases! A common "best practice" is to use the cache to respond to as many requests as possible without touching the database, as well as having a *smart* load balancer that acts as a *firewall* – it's programmed to bounce off most suspicious requests on its own before they touch the server.

A more sophisticated form of DoS is called DDoS (pronounced *dee-dos*), which refers to "Distributed Denial of Service." Instead of sending all the traffic from a single source (which can easily be identified and blocked as we saw above), the attacker creates a large network of *distributed* nodes, making it much harder to see which nodes are legit users and which ones are nefarious.

It's very hard to counter a well-coordinated DDoS attack by yourself, but most of the general guidelines above still apply.

When faced with a DDoS, what you really need is a "big brother" who can push back the bully for you. This big brother has more than enough spare capacity to absorb the traffic, as well as smart infrastructure in place to distinguish different sources of the traffic one by one.

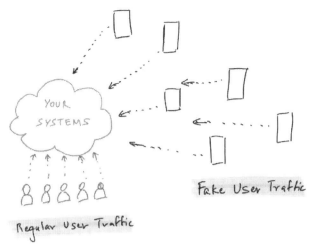

Distributed Denial of Service Attack

Who do you think it is? *Drumroll...* it's cloud computing providers like Google, Amazon, and Microsoft! In fact, at the time of this writing, Google has a specific program called "Project Shield" where they protect small websites (usually independent journalist blogs trying to report on autocratic governments) from repeated DoS attacks, by "adopting" their apps and hosting them on their own infrastructure.

## Closing Thoughts

As computers and software evolve, the ways to compromise them develop in tandem. Therefore, the domain of cyber security is as deep and complex as the entire domain of computer science itself. We could go into more detail like user tracking and authentication (cookies, sessions, tokens, etc), but it's not needed right now.

You've probably seen and enjoyed at least one bank heist, prison break, or Mission Impossible-type movie. These movies are fun to watch because the protagonists solve (or create) one problem after another in very unexpected and imaginative ways. Similarly, you can see how cybersecurity is also a *creative*, almost *artistic* field more than technical.

What's important for you is the ability to take a step back and think like a mischief-maker. When protecting a fortress, first imagine being an invader. It will get better with practice, so keep your naughty hat on at all times!

**Artist: Raquel Paolini Madrid (Venezuela)**

*Scan this artwork like a QR code for optional bonus content.*

Chapter Eight

# Michelangelo Was Probably Goofing

If you were a French aristocrat in the 19th century, dinner for you at a restaurant would have been a long, fancy affair. You would show up wearing your best clothes and proceed to spend the next several hours drinking, gossiping, and dilly-dallying, waiting as chefs prepared one course after another for your culinary pleasure — from a set menu with a fixed price that they decided for you.

The kitchen's environment, however, was the polar opposite from the dining hall. Chefs scrambled to make your dishes in chaos, the atmosphere reeked of cigarette smoke and alcohol (consumed as much by the cooks as the guests), and fistfights breaking out in the middle of service were commonplace.

During this time, along came an enterprising young chef named Auguste Escoffier. He devised a revolutionary way of reorganising the kitchen layout and staff, such that he could trim down the length of dinner from six hours to two. It was called *The Brigade System*, and it was modelled heavily on the strict military hierarchy. Every man had a job, and every job had a man. The kitchen was split up into distinct "stations" – sauces, rotisserie, fryer, desserts, fish, soups, vegetables, bakery, etc. Each station had a *chef de partie* who supervised the cooks under him while reporting to the head-chef and sous-chef above him. There was little tolerance for fistfights, profanity, or disrespect.

With this, the kitchen operated more like a well-oiled machine than a chaotic hubris. Escoffier understood that "time is money" — now he could serve a much broader class of people who couldn't spend half their day socializing, and also offer a much broader, exquisite menu to choose from.

Escoffier became such a legend that Kaiser Wilhem II, the last German Emperor and King of Prussia, personally bestowed upon him an informal title: *The King of Chefs, and Chef of Kings*. Despite modifications over the decades, most modern fine dining restaurant kitchens still follow the spirit of his Brigade System (with a high tolerance for profanity though).

Another big revolution in restaurant operations would come in 1948, when two brothers from California dismantled and rebuilt their restaurant from the ground up, culminating in what they called the "Speedey Service System."

"Speedey" was optimised for speed indeed. Instead of elaborate recipes to be implemented by specialized chefs, they focused on a small menu with simple dishes and mechanized the cooking to focus on consistency and repeatability. They also completely eliminated any need for skilled cooks in their kitchen altogether. The kitchen looked more like a Henry Ford assembly line, where each worker would perform a single step of a process that produced a finished, packaged dish at the end. Guests would have their order serviced in 60 seconds, which was otherwise unthinkable at the time.

This was the birth of fast food, and the two gentlemen went by the legendary name of McDonald which I'm sure you are familiar with.

What's fascinating about these stories is that there was nothing special about the food itself. It could easily be made by anyone else. It was the innovation *behind* the curtain that changed the game.

Software systems are no exception. I've already mentioned in Chapter Four that a solid technical architecture is a necessity while building complex products, because it helps you save a lot of time, money, and confusion. But these benefits only scrape the surface. Smart system design can also set you up for increased productivity, efficiency, and tremendous competitive advantage that pays dividends long after the system is built and the project is over!

We've arrived at a crucial milestone in the journey: you have a fairly intuitive understanding of system design and software engineering, how to scale databases and services, and how to make your company more secure by anticipating how hackers could attack it.

Now it's time to bring it all together, and learn how to actually go about designing and analysing software products and systems at a high level, step by step. I'll also introduce some critical technical topics like microservices. As a continuation of the things we discussed in Chapter Four, instead of the high-level, strategic aspects of engineering, we'll talk about the nitty-gritty.

# A Test Drive

Let's say we decide to build a digital food delivery business. It's a good example to use for our discussion – it has both software and physical systems involved, as well as multiple types of users and stakeholders.

We'll draw up a high-level system design, going all the way from the business plan to the building blocks of the back-end, front-end(s), and the "services" or APIs we'd need.

First, we have the marketing work of identifying who our target customers are, what they care about, how we could best help them better than the alternatives, etc. I'll skip over this because that's outside the scope of this book.

Let's say we decide that our target market will be busy professionals in the city who need to order lunch throughout the week, but don't like to spend time choosing. They'd rather have someone else choose on their behalf and order automatically so they don't have to think about it.

Thinking more deeply about the business model, say we decide to partner with restaurants to make the food because we don't want the overhead of cooking it ourselves. This would be great news for restaurants too – if they can get a week's worth of orders placed ahead of time, it would take out a lot of guesswork from their planning and save them money.

Keeping the interests of all stakeholders in mind (customers and restaurants), we begin to craft the list of high-level features of our service or product.

Let's say we arrive at the following ideas:

1.  Customers can share their food preferences, allergies, major dietary restrictions, and desired quantities.

2.  Customers pay us for a whole week or the whole month.

3.  Customers don't have to decide their meal plan for the week; we do it for them based on their preferences.

4.  Every restaurant gets a full list of orders from us at the beginning of the week, and gets paid by us on a set schedule every week or so.

## A Slight Mindset Shift

As you read through this list, notice that these aren't necessarily features of an *app.* They're features of a *business* that can be packaged into an app if need be. Big difference!

Many managers find the following approach to be the most intuitive: describe to the engineers exactly what kind of app they want to build in excruciating detail, including their strong opinions and instructions on how certain functions ought to be implemented. Give them UX designs and button placement and everything, and let them "go code."

Sometimes they even develop an emotional attachment to their initial idea, like when Michelangelo said these famous words when someone asked him how he makes his sculptures: *"I saw the angel in the marble and carved until I set him free."*

That might have worked for him, but in business terms, it's more like saying, "I envisioned a helicopter schoolbus for my neighbourhood and burned money until my spouse set me free."

Rarely is your first solution your *final* solution. You have to leave some space for iteration and experimentation, especially because there are so many unknowns with technology. As we saw in Chapter Four, one of your jobs is to be a *risk ecologist* – you have to test and validate your assumptions repeatedly. Prematurely picking a solution digs us into a hole from the get-go. This can easily backfire, as you saw in the FBI case study with their 800-page requirements document.

Another thing I'd specifically mention here (which is my personal opinion) is to abstain from doing elaborate UI/UX designs at the very beginning. They should be done before you start building, sure, but only after you've first done some groundwork on the system design and technical architecture. Designing the UI puts you back in Michelangelo mode, which is a stage of development that we want to delay as much as possible.

Don't get me wrong. Often upon hearing an idea for a product or feature, engineers are also tempted to jump straight into talking about how they would build it and the different parts of the technical stack involved and be excited to start coding as soon as possible. The conversation goes all over the place, switching back and forth between minutiae and the big picture until everyone gets lost.

What we want instead is to describe the system at several different levels of abstraction. You want to design the solution layer by layer, holistically, instead of getting lost in the details.

What I'm going to introduce next is a tremendously powerful process that falls under the realm of *Systems Engineering*. Traditionally (by that I mean for more than half a century), it has been an engineering approach that is generally used for the most complex, large-scale, revolutionary projects – think spacecraft, autonomous vehicles, robotic surgery, etc.

Systems Engineering helps you to build the best solution, at the lowest cost, in the most efficient and flexible manner – especially when there are a lot of system requirements, many stakeholders, very diverse teams of experts working together, and the stakes are high.

Now, I have to put a disclaimer. If you look at the Systems Engineering documentation at a big company like NASA, you'll find that it's extensive, follows strict formats, and is very meticulously done. It takes years just to learn how to implement the processes and thinking tools. Not every engineer you'll encounter will have heard of them, especially the types who've just finished a coding bootcamp. So these tools are more for *your* usage, to help *you* get a better understanding of the product or system you're trying to build, than for anyone else's reference.

Furthermore, I've heavily modified these engineering/thinking tools for simplicity, stripping away all the strict rules and formatting to only leave behind the essence. You don't need any software to use these tools; even a pen and napkin are enough. Therefore (and this is where I give you some tough love), it also follows that these are the BARE MINIMUM that you SHOULD be using. These tools are meant to be used; there's zero value in simply learning about them. After you read about them once, go over them again, this time with a pencil and paper, and practice.

## Tool #1: Context Diagrams

The context diagram is a simple, straightforward tool that shows all the high-level stakeholders of your system/business, and the interactions between them.

The first, highest layer is the context diagram. It shows your system as a black box that sits within a larger environment, with your customers and other factors being key stakeholders.

What you do is first define the *boundary* of your system, list everything that it interacts with, and describe the nature of these interactions in "business terms."

In the figure, for instance, you can see a sample context diagram for a company you're familiar with — Airbnb. Notice that it doesn't include any information about technology.

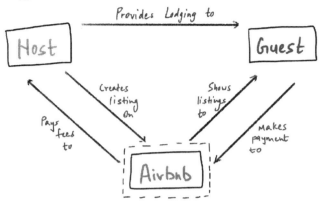

In our case, I will define the following as our core list of stakeholders:

- Customers (who order food)

- Restaurants

- Delivery agents

Here's a context diagram for our food delivery system:

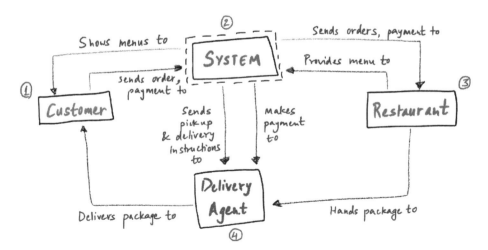

I've kept these diagrams intentionally simple, so they only capture the basics. You can be as detailed as you like, even including regulators, auditors, and all kinds of other external agents (in aerospace context diagrams, you'll find everything from wind to humidity listed as stakeholders). I won't go into details of how to draw this diagram step-by-step. Just get a sense of what it is by looking at the figures.

### Tool #2: Use Cases or User Stories

Your product can have different types of users, and they all need different functionalities. After we've mapped them out in a context diagram, we list out how they will likely use it. We also want to attach a priority level (high/medium/low) to each use case, because we can't build everything for everyone all at once.

In the software industry these are typically called "user stories," which are simple statements that informally describe how and why a user interacts with the product: "As a user of type U, I want to do task T, so that I can solve problem P or get benefit B."

An example story for our app could be, "as a customer, I want to be notified about food deliveries so I can receive them on time."

You can make a list of these in a spreadsheet and assign a priority to them. I want to caution you about something here: in many companies, user stories are the smallest unit of work that are assigned to engineers. This is usually a bad idea. While on the plus side, they're vague enough to give the engineer freedom to make technical decisions and experiment, they're also too vague to be left as they are.

User stories should be treated as just the first level of a *hierarchy of requirements,* which we'll learn about next.

### Tool #3: Functional Requirements and Functional Flow

This concept of *Functional Flow* has been used for decades at aerospace and defense technology companies like NASA, Boeing, Lockheed Martin, etc to build highly complex, safety-critical, ambitious projects. Whether putting a man on the moon or shooting a torpedo in the sea, this is usually one of the first and most critical steps of the engineering process.

Here's how it works. When you're designing a system or process, you always first want to break it down into smaller pieces. There are multiple different ways of doing this breakdown.

The most important one, which I recommend should be done first, is to look at the system simply as a *sequence of functions* it needs to perform in a certain order. Every system, from a food delivery business to a spaceship rocket engine, can be broken down into *a list of things that need to get done* — functional blocks are a universal concept.

This is my favourite part of engineering. It's very dear to my heart and gets me super excited. (I hope that doesn't make me sound like a nerd.)

Here are some examples, in no particular order:

- Get customers' food preferences

- Get information from restaurant menus

- Sort and filter available dishes

- Accept payments

- Place orders for meals at restaurants

- Notify customers

- Deliver the food

- Get customer's feedback

- Make payments

These are the high-level functional blocks of our system. They're like tasks on a to-do list that the system must perform as a whole.

Now here's an essential point: When you're defining the functional flow, you don't care about *how* you will perform or implement those functions. They are technology agnostic – it doesn't matter whether an item on the list will be done using software or hardware or cattle power. You also don't care about inputs/outputs, but only *what* needs to be done.

At the functional design stage, what we're looking for in the end is a *Functional Flow Block Diagram* (FFBD), which is like a flow chart. It includes the main events and conditional logic that make your system work. Here's a sample:

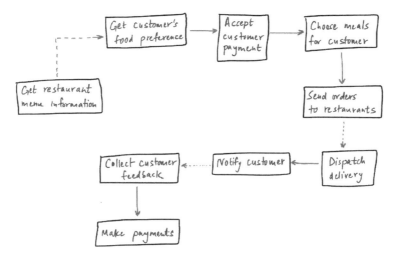

(A dotted arrow represents a potential time lag, and solid arrows mean that the functions are executed immediately after each other.)

This FFBD is very high level, but you can go deeper and be much more granular.

Do not be deceived by the apparent simplicity or "obviousness" of this diagram! And do not skip this exercise when you're building something new. I'd argue that even if an engineer on your team thinks they don't need these things because they're very experienced (an unlikely combination, but you never know), you should draw one for your own sake.

Starting with a flexible, high-level *functional* view of your system pays incredible dividends later on, which may not be apparent to you at this point. We will constantly refer back to functional blocks in later chapters, whether we discuss databases and scalability, cybersecurity, innovating with new technologies like A.I., etc.

Ignoring the technical implementation details, and focusing on what's being accomplished by the system instead, helps bake the "student of your trade" mindset into your engineering process. For example, Netflix changed from a DVD-by-mail service into a predominant streaming service — yet many of their high-level *functional* blocks remained the same. Here are some rough examples:

- Create a list of recommended movies for viewer.

- Allow viewer to search for information.

- Deliver movie to viewer.

You might begin to see how being flexible about your features, and thinking *functionally* instead, can be incredibly valuable.

A side note here: thinking functionally is a muscle, and it takes practice. I've never coached anyone who could intuitively do it from the get-go. But after doing it a couple of times, it becomes much easier. As an exercise, I recommend drawing up a rough context diagram and functional flow diagram for 2-3 tech products that you admire. (I know it's unlikely that you'll sit down to do this even though I just told you, but hey, it's my job to insist once.)

## Tool #4: Non-functional Requirements

For a moment, consider a ride-sharing service like Uber or Lyft, specifically the function of matching a passenger with a driver. How do you decide who gets matched? If you match the passenger with a driver who's 20 minutes away (when there are others available nearby), that would naturally be bad. Moreover, you want to prioritize drivers going in the same direction as the passenger's destination.

If you want, you could drill down even further, taking new factors into consideration: prioritise expensive cars over cheaper cars (if you want to offer a luxury experience), or prioritise drivers that the customer has already ridden with before and given a 5-star rating (it would be pretty cool).

The functional blocks we saw earlier were intentionally quite plain and devoid of details. It's possible to build a system that performs all the "functions," but is still non-functional. This brings us to an additional layer of requirements on top of the functional blocks, aptly called *non-functional requirements*. You could say they give more "texture" to the functions being performed.

In another example, some eCommerce and hotel-booking websites face the problem of abandoned orders simply because of a long, complicated checkout process. So a good NFR might be something like *"it should take less than three steps, and at most eight form fields (including credit card form) to confirm an order once a person clicks on Book Now."*

On the contrary, in the banking industry, security and compliance features are often more important than quick checkouts. And in the autonomous vehicles industry where I'm from, it's usually about safety first.

As you can see, you have to spend time coming up with NFRs that make sense for your system. NFRs are subjective and subject to change based on your strategic plans. It's also easy to get carried away with them and keep sweating the small stuff, making a long dream list of requirements that aren't needed. That's also a no-no. If you try to make your system work perfectly for everyone to use in every way, it will still be under development when your great-grandchildren book their summer vacation tickets to the Moon.

But in any case, ideally you shouldn't expect the engineers to make these decisions on their own. These should be made by whoever is the voice of customers, not necessarily the techies. This is ESPECIALLY important if you're outsourcing the development to a third party.

For our food-delivery biz, say we write these NFRs (I've written them informally here, but you can be more formal if you want):

- Customers can share preferences, but mainly in terms of whether they're vegetarian, vegan or not. They can't get as granular as allergies, not liking particular ingredients, etc.

    This is primarily because having to filter dishes by individual *ingredients* is a TOUGH challenge. No restaurant would keep that level of granular information about all recipes up-to-date, and we're inviting lawsuits if we claim otherwise and make a mistake. (And if someone's an overly sensitive and picky eater, maybe they're not our target customer at this early stage.)

- Restaurants get their payments cumulatively once every 2 weeks, no more, no less.

    Let's say it's because we want to reduce the number of invoices, receipts and bank transfers we deal with, while still providing a level of comfortable, predictable revenue to partnered restaurants.

Next, we'll discuss how you actually *implement* functional and non-functional requirements.

**Tool #5: Structural Blocks**

In the previous section we looked at our functional blocks and how we'd like them to flow. That was the flowchart of our system: *Do this, then do that.*

The *structural* breakdown of the system is different. We again split up the system into smaller pieces, but instead of representing functions to be performed, we'll see them as building blocks: *This thing goes here, that thing goes there.* These building blocks work *together* to perform a single function, by sharing responsibilities, and exchanging inputs and outputs.

In other words, functional flow is like the script of a movie, which describes what happens. It's very intuitive to think of a movie as a sequence of scenes, but when it comes to actually directing and producing the film, you have to start seeing the movie as made up of all the actors and props who interact with each other as governed by the script! These actors are the structural blocks of the movie.

Similarly, while it's okay to think of a product or system as a list of *features,* from an engineering standpoint, you should instead think of a system as made up of smaller subsystems and structural blocks that are used to *implement* the features.

To put this into more common technical terms, I'll introduce the concept of "services."

## Splitting into Services

In 2003, a McDonald's franchisee in Colorado, USA made a small dent in the fast-food universe.

Steve Bigari owned a chain of McDonald's restaurants with *drive-thrus*, and was dissatisfied with some of the bottlenecks in his business. People who love hamburgers didn't like the wait times and mistakes that often occurred at drive-thrus — a single mishandled order could stall the whole line of cars, frustrating both staff and customers.

Although drive-thrus are the very epitome of "fast food," Steve figured out a way to reduce his average order processing time to less than *half* of the nationwide average for McDonald's, to 1 minute 5 seconds as opposed to 2 minutes 36 seconds. While also reducing mistakes in orders!

To do so, he implemented a range of innovations — among them, robotic French fry makers — but the biggest was to *separate the order handling* from the restaurant entirely, and outsource them to a call center instead. You would speak to the order taker on a speakerphone, and also have your picture taken. This would get forwarded to the kitchen and pickup window, to ensure that you get exactly the order you asked for.

As soon as word spread, he had restaurants from across the country asking to borrow his system, which he did — he expanded the call center and started processing tens of thousands of orders a day, 24 hours a day. By making the order-taking an independent, self-contained service, he transformed his business and others'.

Notice that for this to work, the service must be *truly independent* — they had to design the protocol such that a call center operator would NEVER need to talk to kitchen staff on the phone (which would introduce more confusion and subjectivity).

They could only communicate via the order information that appeared on the screen in the set format.

Which would you rather prefer: a wardrobe with T-shirts and trousers, or a wardrobe full of onesies and bathrobes? And why?

One advantage of having shirts, trousers, shorts, etc is that it makes your clothing more flexible and modular. You can switch things up, and if you spill food on your shirt and it needs to go for dry cleaning, the trouser doesn't have to go with it.

One advantage of onesies is that when both the top and bottom are one, it makes things *simpler*. Neat and sorted, no confusion, no hassle.

Think of this as building with Lego bricks.

Keeping components independent and *decoupled* from each other (in tech discussions, you often hear the term "decoupled") is very helpful, because it keeps our system more flexible to changes and innovation. It also helps you find bottlenecks and individually fix, replace or scale up parts of your system as needed. If one thing breaks, the whole system doesn't necessarily go down.

How you break things up is highly subjective, but there are also many design patterns and best practices that you could follow. In the following figure, I show some rough structural blocks that might make sense for our food delivery business:

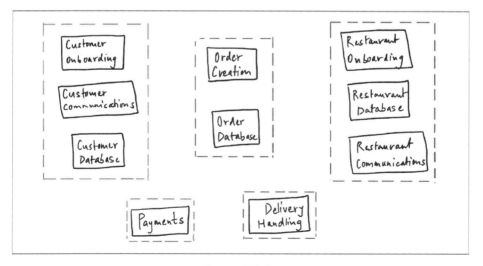

Structural Blocks

For illustration purposes, you can see how I've made several architectural decisions just by defining blocks in this way. For instance, notice that Customer Onboarding and Customer Communications are separate blocks. This is because I foresee them to evolve very differently from each other (the Communications module will probably include complaint handling and other things), so I just keep these blocks of functionalities independent from the start. I do the same for restaurants. I also keep the Payments module separate. Another thing to note is that the databases of customers, orders, and restaurants are not placed *within* any other structural blocks, but kept as separate entities.

Again, this is all subjective. It's good to go through various iterations and take into account the opinions of various team members before you move forward with your architecture.

## Microservice Architectures and APIs

As you split services up into smaller independent ones, you get to *microservices*. This is as opposed to a *monolith*, where a single large block performs many functions by itself.

One company that went all-in on adopting a "microservice architecture" is Netflix. Everything that happens while you're browsing or watching things is controlled by one of several hundred microservices, each of which has its own code and runs on its own little piece of the infrastructure.

Loading your profile picture, storing your browsing history, deducting a monthly payment from your credit card, looking at your browsing history and finding shows to recommend, displaying those shows on your dashboard — each of these functions is performed by a separate microservice that communicates with others via APIs. Whenever you make a *request* to the Netflix backend (by clicking a button, etc), it sends ripples across the system, with hundreds of microservices exchanging data among each other to prepare the response.

One of the biggest proponents of the shift towards API-driven services architectures was Jeff Bezos, the founder and former CEO of Amazon. In 2002, he issued an eyebrow-raising mandate to all of Amazon's development teams, which became a hot topic of discussion all around the tech industry.

Here's the gist of what it said:

1.  Anything that any team built was to be packaged as a service.

2.   Services could only communicate with each other through *APIs*. No other form of inter-process communication was allowed. No exceptions.

3.   All services were also to be designed to be "externalizable," i.e. they could be exposed to the outside world and other developers could use them. No exceptions.

The extended advantages of this were incredible. Four years later, when they launched Amazon Web Services (AWS), they could easily take the services they had developed internally (such as their database systems) and sell them to other companies! Customers could take advantage of the hard technical problems Amazon employees had already solved, and Amazon could squeeze the maximum value from their investment into tech development. But for this strategy to work, you had to have independent, API-based services.

By the way, it's not like microservices are a silver bullet. They also come with issues which may or may not apply to your business. When everything is split into independent units, the flexibility gains are accompanied by a rise in complexity and the need for additional tools (for monitoring, maintenance, etc), which may not be right for an early-stage business or idea.

But that's not for you to worry about. You now have enough of an intuitive high-level understanding that you can let the engineers make the specific decisions and ask them good questions whenever need be. What I don't want is for you to have no idea what the architecture for your company's products and systems looks like or how it works.

———◆———

## From Architecture to Design

In the design stage, we decide on the technologies we'll use and other details. At this point in the journey, some people jump straight to the fanciest possible technology they could use. Don't do that. Not all parts of your system need to be high-tech and fancy. Also, carefully consider the "build vs buy" decision. Don't go building everything on your own unless you have a solid reason to do so.

Take payments as an example. When Pierre Omidyar started eBay in 1995, he just wanted to create an auction website that would help his girlfriend buy and sell candy dispensers online (she was an avid collector). The website soon got a lot of traction from collectors of all kinds of things, so it became expensive to manage. He decided to charge sellers a commission for successful auctions — and his only way of collecting payments was to receive physical checks in the mail. Instead of setting out to build a digital payments system, he focused on improving the website in other ways. Very quickly, he was getting hundreds of paper checks in the mail every month — so many that he often didn't even have time to cash them. Ultimately, they were saved by Paypal which provided them with a robust payments infrastructure.

Another company that's had payment woes is Airbnb, but they took a different approach. Some people don't consider them to be a true "technology company," but that is far from true. While most companies use 3rd-party vendors to handle payments, Airbnb has a huge in-house operation for payments alone, and built their own stack to deal with the complexities of multiple currencies and highly-fragmented payment landscapes in 190+ countries. In some regions, they've even had to find a middle-ground between online payments and cash handovers — all the while also dealing with local compliance, taxation, and financial reporting.

Airbnb's payments operation is big enough that they've spun it out as a subsidiary company called Airbnb Payments (making it decoupled from the main business also helps from a legal standpoint). But funnily enough, they too started out simply using Paypal to get paid by guests and sent hosts a check in the mail until Brian Chesky, the founder, got tired of writing checks by hand. By the way, Brian and his co-founder Joe Gebbia were both "non-technical." They studied fine arts and design.

Steve Bigari, the entrepreneur mentioned earlier who introduced a call center to McDonalds' drive-thrus, eventually evolved that service further with AI. Each customer would first speak to an AI voice assistant, and if the AI assistant *couldn't* handle the order, they would be transferred to a human being at a call center.

A great rule of thumb is to always start small and test a rough solution (at least for back-end stuff) before you dedicate a lot of time, money, and effort to build a robust and elegant tech stack. Look at each functional or structural block, and ask yourself: "Do we really need to create fancy custom software to make this work, and do we need it immediately? Can we use something else that works well enough to let us focus on more important things?" As we discussed in Chapter Four, this decision should be informed by which stage you're at in your validation journey.

## Fat Client, Thin Client

While our focus has mainly been on back-end operations, we shouldn't forget that a lot of modern software also has a front-end user interface (UI).

Of course, not all software needs a UI. An (evil) example is a computer virus. If your computer gets infected with one, it will run completely in the background as it manipulates your data, and not do anything that brings visual attention to it.

There also exists a whole branch of software whose only job is to get the computer hardware to render visuals on the screen, by manipulating pixels. It builds and modifies the Graphical User Interface (GUI) of the software. This is the field of computer graphics, which, surprisingly, started in the 1960s at Boeing, the aircraft company.

If you recall Chapter 3, every software application is a recipe that must be executed on a computer's hardware (kitchen). The hardware can be yours, or it can be the client's.

Depending on the application you're building, you have to decide how much processing needs to happen on your hardware (on the back-end), and how much should happen on the front-end.

This brings us to the concept of a "fat client" and a "thin client." You can probably guess that a fat client means the device can do a lot of processing, independently from the back-end. An example would be your smartphone or personal computer.

In the 70s, when there were no personal computers, most devices were thin clients. You had "terminal devices" through which you could input commands and see outputs, but the real processing happened on an expensive "mainframe" computer.

With the rise of personal computing, this equation flipped – now, most software began to run on fat clients. You could install software using DVDs and floppy drives, or at most, download the file from the internet and install it like that. Beyond that, there was little or no exchange of data with a remote server.

The landscape is slowly changing again, and a lot more of our work happens "in the cloud." Let's look at the different types of applications more closely.

## Static vs. Dynamic Web Applications

In web applications (which run on a web browser), the code that builds the GUI is written in two languages, HTML and CSS – they set up the structure of the webpage and its colours, spacing, styling, and whatnot. Everything that you see is described with HTML and CSS. The browser sees this code as the description/recipe/instruction manual for how to create the painting that is your web page.

A web app's front-end can be made exclusively with HTML and CSS. Some apps' front-end also includes code that changes the HTML and CSS again and again — it makes the app more interactive. On the web, this is usually written in a language called JavaScript or one of its variants (you may encounter words like TypeScript, CoffeeScript, etc).

The above web pages are called static web apps. They use HTML, CSS and JavaScript to do everything right on the front-end. This means, that once your browser has the code, it doesn't need to communicate with a back-end server or a database – you might as well turn off the internet but the web application would still "work."

On the other hand, we have dynamic web apps. They keep sending or receiving data from the server, without which the front-end code is not sufficient.

For example,

- When you're watching a video on YouTube or Netflix, it "buffers" piece by piece and also reduces the video resolution depending on how slow your internet is.

- When you're using Facebook or Instagram, simply by scrolling down it reveals more and more posts and also sends you new messages without having to reload the whole page.

- When you're using Google Maps, whenever you search for a new city it simply moves the map to that location and loads its information, instead of having to download the whole map of the Earth from the beginning.

In all these cases, the browser receives the front-end just once and then keeps receiving more data from the back-end in small chunks.

Most of the applications we use today wouldn't function if they weren't connected to the internet. (This also has implications on scalability and cybersecurity, which you'll be able to better appreciate after reading this book.)

## Non-Web Applications

Non-web applications – which include all software that isn't a website – are installed directly on the operating system (OS) of the device, i.e. on a fat client. Therefore the front-end could be written in many different languages depending on the OS.

Although you already know this, it's worth mentioning again that fat clients range from handheld calculators to arcade game machines to early Nokia phones to modern laptops and mobiles, even smart ovens.

These are often referred to as native applications (especially in the context of mobile apps). They may still be static or dynamic and communicate with a back-end, but they are "native" because they don't need a web browser.

A lot of software can exist both as web and native applications. For example, you can download the Gmail, Facebook, or Netflix app on your phone and also use the website.

Along the same lines, Google Sheets exists only on a web browser, while Microsoft Excel exists mainly as a native app (only recently released in a web-based format in Office 365) and can be used without the internet. Zoom runs natively (it's installed on the device), while Google Hangouts can run in the browser.

Since native apps can directly access the computation resources ("kitchen") of a computer, the same app, if written in both web and native formats, will usually be faster when it's native, because it can access more of the computer's resources than a web browser allows.

Many online multiplayer games (such as Dota2, World of Warcraft, etc) are also native applications that require heavy computation (for graphics, etc) and are installed on the OS. At the same time, if your computer is connected to a network, they allow you to play with other people.

As a downside however, you can't automatically install updates to a native app on a device, without the client's permission! Updating the front-end is easy when your app is web-based, because it's all in your control. There are always trade-offs.

Finally, we come to an interesting related topic.

## The Battle of Programming Languages

For a long time, most non-web applications' front-ends were written completely in C or C++. Then other popular languages like Python and Java came along.

Initially, Android phone apps were written mainly in Java, and iPhone apps were written in Objective-C (because the respective operating systems only supported these languages). Over time, Android began to support a new language called "Kotlin" and Apple came out with its own language called "Swift."

You may be wondering why. Let's do a thought experiment.

If a company wanted to have both an Android and an iOS app, it would have to find a way to translate the front-end code into the respective language. The same goes for any other device.

Recall that "installing software on a device" means getting its code on the device and testing that it's working alright on the device's operating system.

Consider this question - if you were Google and wanted Android to be the most popular mobile OS, a big part of it would be to try to have the greatest variety of apps available that run on each OS.

To get the most number of apps, you would need the most number of developers willing to build those apps.

Now let's say a dev wants to build and sell a mobile game. She has a choice whether to build it for Android, iOS, or any other phone OS. She considers several factors, such as "how many people have Android or iOS phones?", "which platform's apps are the easiest to build," etc. It might seem obvious to you *today* to "build for both," but you haven't considered all the other dozens of potential phone platforms available!

The first question (how many users) is a chicken-egg circle: more apps bring more users, more users bring more developers; and more developers bring more apps!

So for Google and Apple to compete, they also need to focus on other factors - such as the ease of building apps for their platforms.

That's exactly why many of these tech companies – including Facebook, Twitter, etc – invest a lot into building developer-friendly tools and platforms. They know that they're big enough to be an ecosystem, and no ecosystem can thrive without lots of 3rd-party apps being built on top of it. (Although Facebook did kill a lot of clunky quiz apps and games like Farmville back in the day, so there's that.)

How does this affect you? Your choice of the right languages, frameworks, and tools can have more far-reaching effects than just whether it's the best choice for your project.

If a company is using a difficult or obscure language/technology, they won't be able to find enough engineers to work there. For example, more than 95% of the world's ATMs run on COBOL, a 60-year-old language that most developers today don't know how to use.

This can also be a blessing in disguise – Jane Street, a high-frequency trading firm, is known to use OCaml for everything. It's a nice language with many benefits (eg:

being easy to read and understand by traders who aren't programmers), but they originally started using the language simply because one of their early developers convinced the team to use it! Over time, it became an interesting recruiting tool for them because now they're seen as *the company* to work at for all OCaml enthusiasts (when someone's that "enthusiastic" about a relatively obscure programming language, they're probably good at what they do).

Choosing the right technology decision should depend firstly on the requirements of the system you are building. The right frameworks can make recruiting for talent easier, and can also help create a thriving developer platform in the future if needed.

———◆———

**Summary:**

1.  Smart system design is a tremendous advantage. Even for two tech products that do exactly the same thing from the outside, their internal architecture can decide which one gets crippled and which thrives for the long-term.

2.  Don't get attached to a design or idea for how things should work. If anything, get attached to the problem you want to solve or the result you want to achieve. The solution can always evolve.

3.  A good process for making smart decisions is better and more reliable than a hundred isolated smart decisions. By using some simple, time-tested systems engineering concepts, you can erase many blind spots and greatly increase chances of success from the get go.

4.  Always design and describe systems "layer by layer" — stay at one level of abstraction before another, starting with the highest. Context diagram, then functional flow, then structural blocks, and so on.

5.  Don't eat at fast food restaurants. Regardless of what they say, they don't clean equipment regularly and have no incentive to care about hygiene. (Okay, this is just my personal opinion, but it's my book and I couldn't help but include it here, ha.)

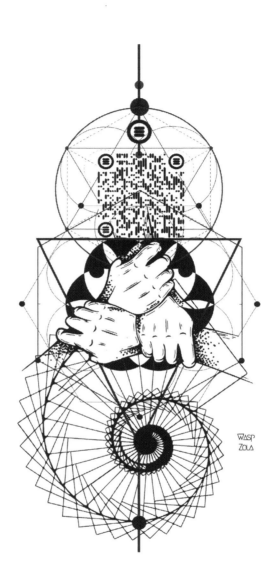

**Artist: Sophie Pakeliani (Georgia)**

*Scan this artwork like a QR code for optional bonus content.*

INTERLUDE III

# *Shock and Cheese:*
# *The Ultimate Product Roadmapping Tool*

When building products and systems, one of the most important things to decide upon is the *roadmap*: what you will build and release first, which features and/or bugs get prioritized or deprioritized, and also which technologies you will use to implement various functional requirements. To help you make these decisions, let me introduce the "Shock and Cheese" framework.

There's a story of a science experiment supposedly done at Columbia University many decades ago:

- They put a hungry *rat* inside a long cage-like device, and placed some *cheese* on the other end of the cage.

- In order to discourage the rat from getting to the cheese straight away, they had an electric grid running between them on the floor.

- The rat would receive a shock whenever it tried to cross over the grid to get the cheese.

The question arose, how much shock would the rat be willing to suffer, to get to the cheese? And could you increase the rat's willingness to bear heavier and heavier shocks, if you just added enough cheese?

Unfortunately, I don't know the results of that experiment, but it doesn't matter for our purposes. It gives us a wonderful parallel for product management and business. Whenever a user or customer uses any application, product, or service, they are looking to get some cheese, but before they can get to it, they have to overcome some shock, which includes ALL the friction they encounter.

- You use Netflix to entertain yourself with movies and TV shows. But you have to connect to the internet with a device, buy a subscription with money, browse the application, decide what to watch and hit play, etc.

- You use food delivery apps just to get food at home, but again have to browse the app, process a payment, and wait for the food to be delivered. A few years ago, you had to call them on the phone and have a conversation to place the order.

- In some countries, to get divorced, you may have to fill out an encyclopedia-thick stack of paperwork and go through many other hoops first. Depending on who you ask, that's a lot of shock in the way of cheese. (According to a French proverb, *"Marriage is like a fortress besieged – those who are outside want to get in, and those who are inside want to get out."*)

Whatever you do with your product or service — adding new features, making things look more beautiful, investing in more security, scalability, "refactoring" code, etc. — will either increase the cheese or reduce the shock/friction for customers.

Quick clarification here: when I say "cheese," it's *not* the same as the "value proposition" of your product. Cheese is simply what the product *does* or *gets* for the user. The value proposition is in finding the *right balance* of shock and cheese.

Digital banks mostly offer the same cheese as a good old regular bank, so their value proposition lies almost entirely in reducing shock instead. Zoom as a software gives you the same cheese as the hundred other video conferencing tools — being able to see and hear the other person. But it greatly reduces the friction caused by them.

On the other hand, when Uber first tested their service in San Francisco, it had more cheese than a regular cab service — a car that *came to you* — but a lot of shock as well! You had to personally email the founders for access, and book rides via SMS messages instead of the seamless app most consumers are familiar with today.

Craigslist, one of the biggest peer-to-peer classifieds websites in the world, also has a user interface that hasn't changed much since the 90s. But they don't care – love it or hate it, their UI is clean and relatable, and it works. Making the site look more beautiful wouldn't help significantly reduce the friction.

Building the right features in the right order ties back to being a student of your trade. Is your product's current problem a lack of cheese to draw users to, or too much shock preventing them from accessing the functionality?

While there is no formula for deciding what goes first, many teams have also found success taking a relentlessly data-driven approach to support this process. Priceline Group, the biggest online travel agency conglomerate that owns everything from Booking.com to Kayak, used to do hundreds of little "A/B tests" all year long: they'd change a small button from yellow to green and see which one caused a higher click-rate, change a few words on the booking page to see how it would affect cart abandonments, etc. Along the same vein, Tripadvisor did a lot of "404 experiments" in its early days – to see if a new feature was worth building in the first place, they'd just create a dead link and track how many people clicked it!

That being said, there's also a risk involved in "stuffing your head into the sand of data" – being too analytical can make you ignore the obvious facts. Facebook's growth team, in its early days, was trying to reduce their churn – some people would create an account, but then become inactive. Instead of finding the perfect medley of small interventions to increase retention (by changing button colors or spamming people with a million emails reminding them to come back to Facebook), Mark Zuckerberg saw the obvious reason: if your friends aren't on Facebook, you won't be back. Being able to see what your friends are up to is really the "cheese" on Facebook. So their onboarding flow focused more on helping people either find their friends or to invite their friends to sign up.

This framework also helps a lot with people management. Often in a team, when you prioritize a project or feature or whatever, you're also prioritizing someone's idea/ proposal at the cost of someone else's. That team member can feel bad, even if that's totally not your intention. The problem arises when you say "no" without a good justification. Having this framework will help you better explain your decision to the team (and to yourself) about *why* certain things are not a priority at the moment.

———◆———

Chapter Nine

# Inside a Dev Org: Turning Chaos Into Code

We've talked about how to properly design software systems and what to keep in mind while leading and managing software projects.

Now, we'll see how things are orchestrated on a day-to-day basis in a typical software team. We'll focus on the miscellaneous steps, processes, and tools involved in building and releasing a piece of software to the world. These topics are a critical dimension of building digital technologies and an essential part of developers' everyday conversations with each other.

## Version Control

I like to see software development as a team of authors contributing to a novel all at once.

At any moment in time, you simultaneously have many parts of the book being written. Some pages may be in the draft stage, some closer to completion. Moreover, the authors would usually rewrite a page/chapter multiple times. They constantly want to undo something they've changed, and may even want to restore a chapter to a much older draft. If the authors don't keep a good record of the changes they're making, the process would be much more painful and much less flexible.

In software development too, there's a lot going on, and managing the changes being made by multiple developers is a chaotic process.

So, developers introduced a concept called ***version control.*** There are several standard tools and processes for version control. These processes dictate how most software is written these days.

The most popular tool for this is called **git**. It's rare to find a software company today that does NOT use git. You don't need to fully understand how it works, so I will only give you the five basic concepts:

1.   Repository

2.   Branches

3.   Merging

4.   Commits

5.   Pushing and Pulling changes

In git, a project is like a tree. The entire project folder (containing all the relevant files) is called a ***repository***. A repository is like an intelligent folder – it can track changes in every file and sub-folder within it.

Git is designed to handle changes and be extremely flexible – you can almost always undo or redo something, whether it's a big change or just a small part of the change. If you mess something up, git is your friend.

To make this even more foolproof, you have the feature of ***branches***. Git allows you to have one *master* version of the project (called the *master branch*), and many other versions exist as branches.

Say you are building a game called Tetris 599. You may decide that the *master branch* will have the latest working version of the game. Naturally, you want to save the working version separately before making changes to it because if every engineer starts editing it independently, the game might break and it will be a pain to figure out how to get it working again.

Instead, every engineer is encouraged to *branch off* from the master – which means they make a copy branch that they're free to change as much as they want, without worrying that they could break something.

Once you make the changes on a branch, test that it works well and are confident about it, as the next step, you can have your changes **merged** with the master branch. So you submit a *merge request*, through which other engineers will verify that your code works and won't break anything. This is called code review or peer code review. In some companies, every piece of code that gets submitted has to be checked and approved by more than one engineer to catch mistakes.

Once the peer reviewers accept your merge request, the master branch will reflect all the changes you made. With this done, you can continue to edit your branch and merge updates using the same process. Every engineer can safely improve the master branch and make it better and better.

If two people try to change the exact same thing in their independent ways and want to merge it with the master, git will automatically refuse to merge until both of them figure out among themselves which changes will be merged.

In summary: you have a repository that contains everything in the project, you have a master branch and can make various other branches to make unique changes. You can also merge a branch with the master branch.

Now, let's zoom in on the process where the developer is making small changes to the code until she arrives at something that works. This process can also be chaotic and frustrating – the developer may have to change multiple files, undo/redo stuff, and so on.

This brings us to the concept of **commits**. A commit is a change that you record inside the "ledger" that is git. Git doesn't allow you to automatically undo or redo the last thing you did, it allows you to travel to the last *commit you made*.

Every commit is like a checkpoint or a "stage" of the project. You can easily go back and forth to any checkpoint/stage. So it's not like a text editor where every single change is automatically committed and you can do a Ctrl-Z to undo. You have to tell git precisely what changes you want to commit to the ledger.

So you make one commit after another until you get to a working version. Often, you are doing this on your own computer. You may even want to share your branch with a colleague so that they can make their own changes.

Therefore, you have to **push** your commits to others. Often you simply push it to the cloud, and then the other person **pulls** it (= downloads it) to their own computer. But if you're on an intranet, you can even push it directly to the other person!

They can also try to merge two branches together (among which neither is the master branch). In short, it's all very flexible and you can use it however you want.

So here we have our second summary: instead of making just one big change to the code, ideally, you want to *commit* the changes to store them like checkpoints. You can also *push* the commits to others, and *pull* their commits to yourself. This is how the collaborative process works through git.

Alright, I just drowned you in jargon. But you don't have to memorize anything; just understand the overall story. Feel free to take a break here to review.

Another big question is how to *organize* all the code in your company. Not too dissimilar to the microservices versus monoliths discussion in the last chapter, you can have a "multi-repo" or "mono-repo" setup. In a mono-repo, all the code for every feature is kept in *one* large repository. (You can guess what multi-repo means.)

The way you separate your code doesn't necessarily affect the actual architecture or design of your system; its main effect is on the productivity and efficiency of developers.

Having the entire codebase in a single repository versus multiple repositories affects the complexity of your automated testing and deployment pipelines (integration testing, unit tests, build times, etc.) which you will learn about now.

## Software Testing

We've already established in previous chapters that you always want to test a system before you *deploy* it. Deployment is also referred to as putting it into *production*. I believe the word "deploy" has a military background, while "production" is borrowed from manufacturing lingo (i.e., putting a product design into production). Another term people use is *shipping* (e.g., "ship code"), which comes from international trade.

Usually, all code passes through various stages before it reaches production. First, it's written on a *development* branch (dev), where the developer does some preliminary code testing. Then, it's committed to a *staging* branch where it's prepared for production. This is where most of the hardcore testing takes place, seeing whether the code runs properly by itself and how it affects *other* pieces of the system when it's executed. And finally, it's merged with the production branch (also referred to as "prod").

Now let's recap what we mean by testing.

## Back to the Food Business

The words "software testing" are as vague as "testing a food business." It could mean a thousand different things. You could test the business idea, the recipe, the kitchen tools and processes, the hygiene, the efficiency and speed of the cooking process, the distribution system, the customer service, and even the packaging or promotional ads.

Testing can range from the most minor things to the largest, and you can classify tests in a hundred different ways depending on how you look at it. It's also an *art*. Every company has its own approach to testing. We've already discussed the strategic aspects of testing in Chapter Four; to recap, we learned that testing involves an investment, therefore it has both a cost and an ROI. You want to be cognizant of the ROI.

From your perspective as a leader, all testing falls into two large categories: verification and validation. Verification means testing if the thing works as it's supposed to, and validation means confirming if it's worth building. Everything else is just a detail that deals with the "how." We've already talked about validation testing and the different levels of fidelity of prototypes, so in this chapter, we'll focus on verification.

## Manual vs. Automated

You can test something manually every time, involving a human performing some operations. Or, you could define a test that just happens automatically (conducted by a software program).

If you had an assembly line that produced coffee packets, and there was a risk of some packets being empty (containing just air), an example of an *automated* test would be to fix a powerful fan at the end of the line that simply blows away all empty packets. (You can probably guess what the manual version of such a test would be.)

On the other hand, it's much harder to devise an automated test for the taste or quality of the coffee itself or how the packet sounds when you touch it. Not kidding: in 2008, SunChips came out with compostable packaging that was so noisy, it was as if lightning struck every time someone touched the wrapper; it reached 96 decibels, which is as loud as a lawnmower. Usually, manual testing is reserved more for validation than verification.

## Unit Tests

If I handed you a brand new calculator and asked you to test if it's accurate or not, what would you do? If you're like me, you will make it perform calculations you already know the answers to (5+5, 10-2, and so on). If you wanted to get serious, you'd try more unusual stuff like 100 ÷ 0. But you get the idea. The 100 ÷ 0 is what's called an *edge case* – it shows how well the system works at the "boundaries."

Similarly, when we write some code, it usually takes certain inputs and produces an output. *Unit Testing* means running a piece of code repeatedly with a list of pre-decided inputs and seeing if it consistently produces the expected output. To make it more robust, you try to add as many edge cases as possible.

Many engineers believe that you should write the unit tests *before* you even start writing code, so that you always have some minimum objective criteria to judge the quality of the code. You don't want the engineer to decide how they'll test their own code *after* they've written it!

Once unit tests are written, you can run them automatically, which is good. However, not everything can easily be unit-tested, and if you replace the code completely (or change what it's supposed to do), you also have to rewrite the unit tests too. So it can be a little frustrating sometimes.

Typically, unit tests fall under the umbrella of "smoke testing," which refers to a series of simple and cost-effective tests that you can perform to check if something is even barely functional, before you waste time doing more serious and thorough tests. The term allegedly comes from electronics testing: You plug in a new circuit board, and if you see smoke coming out when you turn on the power, you have the results of the test!

After code reviews, smoke testing is a great way to cheaply reject a lot of bad code before it reaches production.

**Integration Testing**

Most systems — whether a software application or an automobile — are much more likely to break at the *junctions/interfaces between components* than due to a component failing on its own. You could test all the individual parts of a system, and they may work fine, but you still need to put them together and see if the thing works as intended as a whole. So you have to do things like Integration Testing to ensure things work well together. These are the opposite of unit tests.

I will deliberately skip giving you more names of test types because what matters is the *essence*, and you've already got it. Just remember that to save time and money, you usually want to test progressively: individual components, then multiple components, and then the whole system.

Usually, the engineers on your team will have certain types of tests that they're used to doing already (the better the engineer, the more they're aware of the importance of testing). What *you* need to make sure is whether they are on the same page as you regarding the overall risks you're trying to mitigate.

## Building and Deployment

As you may recall, code is usually written in a high-level language meant for humans to understand, not for computers. Computers only understand the lowest of the low, i.e. "binary language" (ones and zeroes). All code is converted into these binary files that a computer can directly use.

The code that programmers write is referred to as *source code.* The binary version of the software is called the *executable* – because it is what's ultimately executed by the computer.

Therefore, you may write 50,000 lines of code for a software project and this code may live in a structured folder with well-organized files, but it is then converted into a few binary files that have nothing to do with how you wrote the high-level code. This conversion is called "building."

A "build" is the result of this building process. It's the final software artifact.

This is convenient because:

- These binary files are usually much smaller than their source code. You don't want people to download gigabytes of code to run the software.

- You don't want people to read your source code! You want to protect the recipe.

Building is an important step in testing and moving your code from dev to staging to prod. You may come across the term "build time," which is the time it takes to build your code. Build times depend on the size and complexity of your code and are an important constraint in company operations.

# Continuous Integration and Delivery (CI/CD)

A lot of companies try to be as *agile* as possible. They want to iterate quickly, which includes speeding up the rate at which you build and test code.

To achieve this, you want that as soon as a developer writes a piece of code that works fine, it gets pushed along the "development pipeline" and is on its way to becoming part of the final product. You *integrate* the code/feature with the product, and then *deliver or iterate* on it, on a *continuous* basis. This is called Continuous Integration and Delivery. As you can imagine, this is just a concept, and companies achieve it to varying degrees.

CI/CD focuses heavily on automating as many steps as possible. There are a plethora of tools available to handle this, such that all a developer has to do is push a commit to the repository, and the CI/CD pipeline does all the smoke testing, integrations, building, etc. on its own and gives feedback to the developer on which tests passed and which ones broke.

You also have "Feature Flags." Sometimes, you've written a feature that isn't quite ready yet, so you don't want it to be the cause for the entire build process failing. So you can use feature flags to turn such features on or off during the CI/CD process.

## The Chaos

We may not realize it, but if you look at the whole picture of a software company from a distance, it can get chaotic.

On the client side, you have so many different devices and types of users. Each device has its specifications (from an old desktop with Windows XP to the latest iPad or Android smartphone). Each web browser has its specifications too. Moreover, the devices are distributed all over the world, and different types of users can have different levels of access to certain features of the same application.

On the back-end, you have numerous services and databases interacting with each other, and with all the clients. Many of these services need to run on different machines that all have their specifications — just like in a commercial kitchen, each "station" needs various equipment. So you could say that the different "pieces" of software have their own *dependencies* and resource requirements. This is especially chronic when you have hundreds or thousands of microservices.

Then you have people with a variety of *skill sets* — from machine learning models to GUI design. Everyone is writing code on different computers, that has to be integrated into one source of truth, and all code has to be tested and checked before it becomes part of the deployed system.

## Developers and Operations

As you can imagine, companies have had to create processes to manage this chaos. A critical part of this process was the emergence of roughly two special buckets of roles in a software company: developers and operations.

Devs include software engineers and other supporting roles who *produce code*. They are the ones who decide which features need to be built and then build them. After that, they'd hand it over to others who handle the logistics of how to get their product *delivered* to customers.

The operations people are typically ultimately responsible for testing, delivery, and scaling. They don't write much code, but they are the ones who greenlight its quality and handle decisions around what kind of infrastructure and platforms the system will run on. They're supposed to decide the "cloud" strategy, etc.

This division of responsibility looks beautiful. Devs churn out code for Ops as their internal customer, and the Ops take care of the rest.

However, when there's a *problem*, the rosy painting we have painted flips from heaven to hell, with a lot of finger-pointing about whose fault it is. If there's a bug in the software, is it the fault of the developers, the testers, or the ones that deployed it? If a microservice crashes, is it the fault of the code running on it or the people managing the infrastructure and making sure it is fault-tolerant?

Then there are power dynamics which vary from company to company — at the end of the day, it is human nature to do the least work possible, so it's natural for one team to demand from the other that they take more responsibility. At best, this causes mutual frustration over things not being smooth. And at worst, this causes a lot of "us vs them" inside software companies, where some teams become siloed and take an adversarial stance against each other. It's a classic example of how culture is shaped by the nature of the work.

## Intro to DevOps

The above was the story of most software companies. Recently, a new "philosophy" emerged, that developers and operations should work together at every step of the way, in a collaborative rather than adversarial fashion. As always, the tech industry has a name for it: *DevOps*.

We've seen that although simple in principle, due to the nature of the work, DevOps is hard in practice. Unless the nature of the work changes, companies will always be swimming against the tide trying to keep all parties happy and cooperative.

Here are two things that can change the nature of someone's work:

• A shift in the responsibilities and structure of work

• The emergence of new tools and technologies

We already saw a glimpse at two such tools: version control and automated testing/building. By giving devs instant test results as soon as they try to push any new code, and more control over the deployment pipeline, they automatically assume responsibility for making fixes without finding someone to blame. (More on this later.)

Another tool that makes DevOps easier is "containerization."

## Containerization

Every software application (from smallest to largest) has certain requirements for running. At the bare minimum, it needs to be translated into machine code and compiled, etc., but at a higher level, it may also have dependencies like specific programming frameworks, libraries, and modules.

All these things are parts of the *environment* of an application. Without this environment, the app/service won't work. Then it also has some hardware requirements (memory, processors, etc.). Without enough of these, either the software won't work or will be too slow.

Now think back to testing and building. When you're testing an app, naturally you want to test how it works in the same environment as where it will eventually be operational. For example: if you're building an app that should be able to work on iOS 11, but you *only* test it up to iOS 10 before launching, there may be some bugs when iOS 11 users use your app! Then, to reduce friction and back-n-forth in the whole process, wouldn't it be simpler if the engineers also used the same environment while *writing* the service?

Therefore, it is usually in the company's best interest to ensure that a piece of code is written, tested, and deployed in an identical environment.

However – an engineer may be building multiple services as part of their job. They also usually have only one computer they use for work, with a fixed RAM, etc., so it's also hard to tweak the actual RAM and processing power available to an app on your laptop.

And *then* – you have multiple engineers working on the same service. All of them may have different computers! In the midst of all this, how do you ensure that everyone in the company can use an identical environment for an application and easily accommodate multiple environments as needed?

The key is containerization. Engineers developed the concept of a "container" that acts as a template for the environment, in which you can define all the dependencies precisely. Then you can recreate that container anywhere.

This is part of a broader concept called *virtualization* – where a single machine can "virtually" run multiple environments simultaneously.

You can make as many copies of the container as you want. You can run multiple different containers on the computer, each completely isolated from the other. You can then also build tools to create, deploy, and manage all these containers automatically.

A term you'll come across quite often is *Docker*. It's the name of a tool that people use to create these containers. Often, people say "docker containers" and "docker ecosystem."

With Docker, you can create and manage containers – you input the specifications of the environment you want the container to run, and Docker gets it done. The developers, testers, and other operations people all use copies of the same container while working with a particular application.

And how do they share the specifications of the containers so that they know how to create the copy? Version control! It makes sure that everyone has the most up-to-date specifications for a particular app's container/environment so they can stay on the same page.

Then, automated testing (particularly CI/CD) removes more friction. When developers continuously push code to production, they'll naturally get to "talk" to the operations folks more often. Therefore, problems get discovered and fixed faster, and more communication equals more cooperation.

This is why many software companies these days have dedicated "DevOps Engineers" whose sole job is to make the development, testing, building, and deployment of software more seamless and scalable. They touch every aspect of the software development process, from enforcing unit tests to setting up containers in the cloud, and also helping with project management. Some companies also have "Site Reliability Engineers" (famously originating at Google), who focus more on the reliable performance of the infrastructure and making sure that apps never go down.

We have two more quick topics before we wrap this up.

## Technical Debt and Refactoring

As we saw in the previous chapters, as you build software iteratively, you can't do everything perfectly all the time. You have to prioritize and deprioritize things, and sometimes have to cut corners, which means that your product or its code always has certain problems that need to be fixed later on. This is especially the case when you follow a highly agile methodology for development and asking developers to release a working version every couple weeks.

This is called "technical debt." It's a broad term that covers many things: bugs, poorly implemented features, security flaws, etc. Whenever you deprioritize something for the short term, you're "borrowing" time that you'll have to pay back later.

One activity that comes up frequently in this category is "refactoring" of code. It doesn't change what the code does, but rather improves how it's designed on the inside – and if you learned anything from Chapter Eight, you know the value of good internal design.

Good engineers will often want to spend a portion of their time getting rid of technical debt, because it makes your codebase healthier over the long term. It might seem like a waste of time because it doesn't result in the creation of any new features, but it's highly advisable.

Consider it akin to doing maintenance and upgrades on a car. You can argue that it's not needed *most* of the time, but if you *never* do it, it will not only hamper the driving experience, but the damage could also pile up quickly.

# Documentation

I could summarize this section in just one sentence, as some of my aerospace peers used to tell me: *"If it ain't documented, it ain't done."*

Documentation can take various forms. At the very least, it includes writing inline comments that explain what a given line of code does. More generally, it's in the form of detailed "readme" files which explain in detail what a module does, how it works and why it was designed the way it was. Many companies also have handbooks that contain the best practices decided by the engineering team and deemed mandatory to follow for all developers.

Fundamentally, the simple practice of *writing things down* and keeping good records of how and why decisions are being made has various benefits, which I'm sure you don't need me to list out. That being said, many engineers (especially the ones who fall into the "agile" camp) find that they're not given enough time to write documentation, or at least their managers don't consider it "productive." Nothing could be further from the truth.

Depending on your business and industry, you can choose how rigorous your documentation needs to be. For instance, if you're building medical software in the European Union, you bet you'll have to keep detailed documentation, or the regulators will come and smack you. You also have to choose which parts of your codebase need the most extensive documentation and which ones are self-explanatory enough. As a rule of thumb, for any core functional module, ask yourself what would happen if the engineers who designed and developed it got hit by a bus tomorrow. You'll know how much documentation that module needs.

——◆——

This chapter may have read like an assortment of miscellaneous topics, but they're all connected. I hope it gave you a more granular "feel" for what software engineering is really like, and how complex these organizations can get.

Besides the testing strategy, you don't need to have strong opinions on most of the things we discussed here; just a general awareness is enough.

**Artist: Ryn Ortega (USA)**

*Scan this artwork like a QR code for optional bonus content.*

Chapter Ten

# Artificial Intelligence: The New Dawn

In 1975, a man named Otis Johnson was sent to prison in the United States for a crime he did not commit. He would eventually get released in 2014, after 44 years of incarceration.

When Johnson was finally let out at Times Square in New York City, instead of feeling free, he stood frozen. He said he was surrounded by CIA agents — "hundreds of them," walking around him everywhere he went — talking into wires in their ears or small walkie-talkies, with blank facial expressions.

*"What's going on?!!"*

Or so he thought. He had no idea that he had, in effect, teleported to a distant future.

Johnson had bypassed the *entire era* of personal computers (Microsoft and Apple hadn't officially started when he entered jail), including mobile phones, the internet, social media, and cat GIFs.

The "CIA agents" around him turned out to be just regular people plugged into their earphones.

This chapter is about artificial intelligence and automation.

Usually, when I talk to people about AI, their questions fall into two broad categories:

- Does AI have feelings, is it going to kill us, will it steal my job, are we doomed, etc, etc.

- How can I use it for my business and make lots of $$$?

The first discussion, while being exciting for sure, often snowballs into an intellectual fortune-telling exercise, which I don't feel qualified to partake in.

At the risk of exaggerating my humility, I'll say that even after studying and observing the developments in this technology for many years and being the host of the Age of AI Podcast (through which I meet more CEOs of AI companies weekly than almost anyone else in the industry), my predictions are as good or bad as anyone else's. They might be good for dinner conversation over a fine bottle of rotten grape juice, but not for this book.

Which brings us to the next common question: how can you use AI?

Surprise, surprise — I might disappoint you again! At the time of writing this book, within the *last 5-7* years alone, AI programs have accomplished feats that experts hadn't predicted happening for the *next* 30 years. They have:

- Beaten human world champions and even entire teams of world champions in various kinds of games, including Poker and Go

- Learned to predict how proteins fold inside a cell (something humans have been trying to do for 50 years)

- Learned to *see through concrete walls,* in absolute darkness, by analyzing the bouncing WiFi signals (!)

- Been able to *read human minds* — directly translating thoughts into synthetic speech by processing brain waves (!!)

- Been able to diagnose certain respiratory and neurodegenerative diseases just by *listening to a patient's voice*

...and I can testify as a former autonomous vehicles engineer that AI can drive a car better than I do.

Let all this sink in for a moment.

For most of human history, any significant technological, geopolitical, and lifestyle changes happened over centuries. In the last few hundred years, similar shifts began occurring over decades. Now, big significant changes are happening *within* decades. The rate of change is faster than ever.

Therefore, I don't see the point in telling you about the *present* bleeding-edge use-cases of AI in the industry for you to cherry-pick and get inspired. I might drop a few examples here and there, but don't let them narrow your imagination. Most of them would be old news within five years.

Instead, I'll focus on helping you understand how this tech works at a fundamental level, *intuitively*. I want to empower you to *follow new developments* in this field by yourself, participate in intelligent conversations, and explore your own creative ideas solving problems using AI.

Now, since AI is one heck of a buzzword and every Tom, Dick, and Harry is peddling a questionable "AI-powered" software product these days, we'll talk more specifically about *Machine Learning* (ML).

You might see a figure or two with some mathematical expressions in them, but don't get scared or give a knee-jerk reaction when you see them – they're extremely basic and for illustration purposes only. There's no complicated math or physics in this chapter.

Let's begin!

## Elephants and Tigers

Let's say you were a wildlife safari enthusiast, and I was your super-idiot friend. I'm going on a safari in Africa next week. So you give me some advice: "Aman, please stay away from the elephants."

And I ask you back, "What's an elephant?"

You might say, "Seriously? Elephants are... okay never mind, here's a *picture* of an elephant; this is what it looks like. Just stay away from them."

Next week you hear that I *still* managed to run into an elephant and almost got myself trampled. You ask me what happened.

"I don't know, I did see this huge animal but it didn't look anything like the photo you showed me, so I thought it was safe to play with and I went ahead and pulled the little wagging thing. Here's the photograph of the animal I took before that..."

You: "...Wow. I'm sorry Aman, my bad. I expected too much from your brain. Let me give you a 'cheat code' which you need to follow when you're on safari next time. If you see anything that looks brown or gray from all angles, seems to have four leathery legs like pillars, large flapping ears, and a long thick nose coming out of its face like a big tube and is fat and bigger than you are, then that's probably an elephant and you need to stay away."

Next month I go back to safari again (hey, it's my hypothetical story and I can go to safari as many times as I want), and I don't run into any elephants this time because your "cheat code" works well enough.

Let's review this story using slightly more *technical* terms.

At first, I had no idea what an elephant was, no mental image or MODEL of what it even looked like. If I was forced to describe an elephant, I'd have said something random, a wild guess.

When you showed me the first picture, suddenly, I was able to construct a clearer mental model of an elephant. I noted many visual FEATURES that stood out to me: big flappy things, the large trunk, the two apparent eyes on each side, the little white tusks, the big long face, and the approximate shape of the body.

If I had *then* seen an animal that had those same features, I'd have guessed with a high degree of CONFIDENCE that it was an elephant.

Unfortunately, since I had only seen a single picture of an elephant, the features I learned were very limited. My mental model could not be GENERALIZED to work on recognizing elephants when seen from different perspectives, lighting, etc.

If I'd had more DATA (more pictures of an elephant from different perspectives), I'd have been able to pick out more unique features and create a better mental model from the get-go.

*However, your* mental model of an elephant was much more generalizable because you had already seen a lot of diverse data. And I could make immediate sense of your cheat code because I already had solid mental models for the features you mentioned: flappy ears, leathery legs, long nose like a tube, etc.

In summary, the more data we get exposed to, and the better we extract unique features from that data that help us see patterns, the better models we can build to help us make decisions easily.

Note that I still didn't really know exactly what an elephant is; I just had a cheat code/model that helped me recognize an elephant based on certain features. (And from a philosophical standpoint — do you *really* know *what* an elephant is? Or don't we all perceive the world through similar cheat code models and judgments? Something to think about.)

Here's another fun example. Have you seen the original *Lion King* movie from 1994?

You might be surprised to learn that there was not a single lion's roar in the entire film. In the recording, they replaced all the lion roars with tiger roars! In the real world, a lion's roar is quite underwhelming – it sounds more like a groan. A tiger's roar is bone-chilling. It has special infrasounds meant to paralyze a victim with fear, giving it the "ferocious and majestic" quality that makes you sit up and take notice — exactly the effect they were looking for.

(If you've seen the MGM lion mascot who showed up at the beginning of Tom and Jerry cartoons and other media, that lion was also dubbed by a tiger for the same reason.)

Most people's mental model of a roar hasn't been TRAINED on enough data, and so we haven't extracted good features that help us distinguish between the sounds of a lion, tiger, or even leopard and jaguar. This concept of "models" is central to machine learning and artificial intelligence.

## Artificial Neural Networks

Let me first introduce to you a special sub-domain of Machine Learning called *Deep Learning*. The basis of deep learning is "artificial neural networks" (ANNs) which I'll describe now.

First, I assume you remember a little bit of math from high school. You know what a matrix is, and that you can multiply a matrix with another matrix? That's it — that's quite literally the ***only*** piece of math I need you to know for this chapter.

Quick visual:

$$\begin{bmatrix} x & y \end{bmatrix} \cdot \begin{bmatrix} u \\ w \end{bmatrix} = xu + yw$$

The human brain is made up of a network of many cells called "neurons," which is the inspiration for ANNs. This is what it looks like on paper:

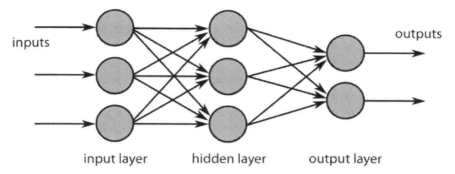

You can assume that each circle you see in this diagram is a neuron or "node" of the NN

The ANN is a mathematical model. It takes an input, processes it through its "cheat code" and gives you an output. This "cheat code" is called the "weights" of the ANN.

You saw that matrix earlier? You can say that the first [x y] matrix is an input, and the second [u w] matrix is the set of *weights* or cheat codes. When you multiply the input with the weights, you get an output.

So the ANN acts as a *model* that has weights *trained* using lots of data to produce intelligent outputs. I will use the terms ANN, network, and model interchangeably.

Next, let me show you just a little bit of what goes on under the hood and how the "training" works, just so you don't think of it as magic. Feel free to skip the section if you find it hard to take in.

But first, take a break and review the concept of a "model" again. If it's still fuzzy, don't worry, we'll keep building that intuition as we go along!

## Training Neural Networks (Optional Reading)

Suppose you wanted to build an ANN which takes in a photograph and tells you if the photograph is of an elephant or not. You put a photo into the box, and out comes an answer "yes" or "no."

Since it's just numerical matrices, you can create ANNs of endless varieties, and based on how you design them, they can either give a "yes or no" answer, or a specific number, or a list of different numbers, etc. You can choose what kind of output the

ANN will give and what kind of input it will receive, and how large and complex it will be, which makes it extremely versatile. You can build neural networks that take videos as inputs, voice samples, images, text, etc.

Of course, all these are converted into numbers that feed into the model, and there will be a huge matrix of "weights" which will be multiplied by that input, generating an output which is your answer.

But I'm sure you don't understand completely. How do you "train" the model with data to give you meaningful outputs?

First, you create a fresh ANN that takes an image as input and gives out a certain type of output. At first, this ANN doesn't really know anything about the problem it's trying to solve. It's just like me from the original elephant example — before you showed me the first photograph of an elephant, I had no idea what an elephant even was.

If you asked me right there and then to look for an elephant in a photograph, I'd probably have picked something randomly. So you can say that initially, I had some *random* bullshit cheat code right? But the moment you show me ONE elephant and tell me that it is an elephant, *suddenly* I adjust my random cheat code and now I have *some* idea of what elephants are. My cheat code is not random anymore, and if I saw an elephant from the front I'd probably pick the right answer! So I *updated* my cheat code when I was given more information. And the more different photographs of elephants I have, the better my cheat code becomes at giving the right answer. I still don't know "what" an elephant is, but I've seen enough correlation in different photographs to recognize the most special features of an elephant and stay away from them.

Similarly, when you first create an ANN, you start by giving it a *random* set of weights (=cheat code) to start with. Then you show it an input image (photograph of an elephant) and also tell it the output you expect (answer "yes"). The beauty of ANNs is that if you give it an example input and its corresponding output, then it will *adjust its cheat code* so that it can repeat that correct answer next time. It will *change the numbers in that matrix of weights* the more data you give to it, to be able to match your answers. This is why you can start with a random set of weights, and with time, the ANN will adjust them so that they work well as a cheat code! Cool right? That's how the ANN "learns." The more data you give it, the more it adjusts its weights and the more accurate it becomes.

As I explained earlier already, how this happens is through matrix multiplication. The matrix of weights for this ANN will have values such that if you multiply it with your input image (the image will be converted into numbers), you can get an answer. Usually, there's not just one matrix of weights, but a series of matrices which you multiply one after the other. But the concept is the same as you see in the image below:

$$\begin{bmatrix} x1, x2, x3 \end{bmatrix} \times \begin{bmatrix} w1, w2, w3, w4, \dots \\ w1, w2, w3, w4, \dots \\ w1, w2, w3, w4, \dots \\ w1, w2, w3, w4, \dots \\ w1, w2, w3, w4, \dots \end{bmatrix} = \begin{bmatrix} \text{Output} \end{bmatrix}$$

INPUT                    WEIGHTS                    ANSWER
(eg: Image of Elephant)        (Cheat Code)            (What you need)

But that's not enough. Remember that the ANN is not smart — it works on cheat codes, after all. If you only gave it a small handful of elephant photographs to look at, and kept saying "yes" for every photo, what do you think it would do?

It will be lazy and assume that *every* photograph is an elephant! It will adjust its weights (cheat code) in such a way that regardless of the photo it is given, it will always output a "yes." This is called *"underfitting"* which basically means you made the mistake of thinking that your idiot friend is smart. Your ANN has become *biased* towards a particular answer.

To prevent this, you need to also feed it counter-examples that have the answer "no." So you also mix in lots of example photos that are not of elephants, but even lions, cows, human beings, squirrels, and pokemon, and now the ANN will be forced to adjust its cheat code more carefully. Now you're increasing its accuracy and making it more reliable! Or, you can also have *"overfitting,"* when the ANN's cheat code is still lazy, but it's now so super smart that it begins to *memorize* the entire training data you give it.

This often happens when your ANN is very large and deep, so in a way it just begins to store all the information you give it. It becomes super good at answering on your training data but it fails when given a new example that it hasn't encountered before. It's no longer working like a cheat code, but rather it has become like a dictionary of images.

You can prevent this by reducing the size of your model (by randomly dropping some of the weights) or by increasing the variety of data. The former is called "dropout" (pretty straightforward but a very crazy idea), and the latter is called *"balancing the dataset."*

You have also learned your lesson from the safari example earlier, and now you will be careful to show it other photographs of elephants from *many different angles* so that it doesn't make the same mistake that your idiot friend made. This is why researchers/ engineers often *"augment"* their training data sets to include mirror reflections or brighter/darker versions of the same images etc., to increase the variety of their data. This helps make sure that the ANN can become as accurate as it can. You want the cheat code to be so super "robust" that it works as well as real humans, or better.

By the end of the training, with enough *balanced* data and augmentation, you will have a trained ANN (also called trained model) which can recognize elephants in images with reasonable accuracy, and also know when *not to recognize* an elephant.

"Overfitting," the term you encountered just two paragraphs ago (=network becoming too smart and acting like it has just memorized your data), is a very common term in the Deep Learning lingo and you now know what it means. (Underfitting is a less troubling problem because it's fairly obvious to diagnose and easy to tackle.) Someone might say, "oh my model isn't working so well on new data, I guess it is overfitting" and you'll say, "did you try to augment the training data?" and you will instantly own the night.

The process of adjusting weights (updating the cheat code based on data) involves something called *backpropagation*. While training, whenever you show the ANN an example input (let's say a kitten) and then tell it the answer ("no it's not an elephant!"), it will first try to use its current cheat code to come up with its own answer.

If the answer is RIGHT, then it doesn't need to adjust its cheat code, right? The lazy ANN will update its cheat code only when it makes a mistake. So only if the ANN's answer was WRONG, it will have to adjust its weights (=cheat code) by a *tiny* bit and test the weights again. The "mistake" made by the ANN sends ripples through the matrix of weights, changing many of their values. So you can say that the error *propagates* back through the network. Again, this is why you can always create the ANN with random weights initially, and over time it will adjust them on its own. This adjustment algorithm is called BACKPROPAGATION.

Put simply, if you take a cheat code to an exam, and get some of your answers wrong, then you will likely upgrade your cheat codes for the next exam in that subject to have higher accuracy. The process of editing/rewriting your cheat code after every exam, based on its grade, is backpropagation.

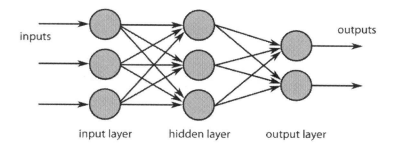

inputs                                                        outputs

input layer          hidden layer          output layer

Look at the graph image of a "neural network" again. You see that thing called the "hidden layer"? Well, the ANN is made of *layers of neurons*, these neurons carry the weights as values. They are called "hidden layers" because you don't need to know the exact weights in the network! You can print the values out, for sure — but it's useless to look at a matrix which can run into millions or billions of small numbers. It's a cheat code, and it updates itself based on the inputs you give it, and that's all you need to know.

This is why deep learning is often considered a "black box" system. If you've ever programmed before in any language, you are used to writing down explicit instructions for the program for everything. But here, you can't see the underlying "cheat code" the computer created for itself to use in place of a written algorithm.

Feel free to take a break, but you don't have to review this section right now; you can do it after you finish the chapter.

## Designing AI Systems

So we've seen what models are and how they're trained.

ML is a great tool for problems where it's "better to show than to tell." That means it would be more convenient to let the computer learn from seeing lots of examples or doing lots of experimentation and learning by doing than to follow a set recipe of instructions in the form of code. This opens up a LOT of room for solutions to problems we couldn't solve earlier with code, and neural networks continue to surprise us with just how much they can "learn" when shown enough examples.

However, this doesn't affect the fundamental processes and tools we learned in Chapter Eight for technical architecture and system design. At the end of the day, even a machine learning model is simply a structural block that takes in certain inputs and produces a certain output. The big difference is that instead of writing code, you are creating entities that can learn on their own and create their own instructions.

Now, I want to share a case study on how to use AI models, specifically deep neural networks, to create powerful structural blocks. The goal here is to give you a feel for *how to think in terms of "models"* and use them in creative ways to solve problems. It's also optional to read, so you can skip to the end of the chapter if you want to, but I recommend going through it because it's a fascinating story!

# How an AI Program Changed Humanity Forever (Optional Reading)

Go is an ancient strategy board game that has existed for over 2,500 years in East Asia. It has so many possible moves at each step that future positions are hard to predict, so most people use strong intuition and abstract thinking to play. For this reason, it was believed that only humans could be good at playing Go, and most researchers thought that it would still take decades to build an AI which could think like that.

But in 2016, Google's recently acquired AI research lab, DeepMind, unveiled a program called "AlphaGo" which shook the world by defeating one of the best players in the world, Lee Sedol.

But AlphaGo didn't stop there. Eight months later, it played 60 professional games on a Go website under disguise as a player named "Master," and *won every single game,* against *dozens* of world champions, that too without resting between games. Naturally, this was a HUGE achievement and sparked worldwide discussions about whether we should be excited or worried about AI.

Three years later, Lee Sedol retired from professional Go, saying that even if he indeed became the number one player in the world, AI was an entity that could not be defeated.

Let's go over the basics of how AlphaGo worked. You don't need to know how to play Go to understand it; you just have to know what a 2-player board game is, in which each player takes turns and there is one winner at the end.

## The Basics

To explain AlphaGo, let me first talk about something similar done for Chess. In the early 1990s, IBM came out with the Deep Blue computer which defeated the great champion Garry Kasparov in Chess. How did Deep Blue play?

Well, it used a very brute force method. At each step of the game, it took a look at all the possible legal moves that could be played, and went ahead to explore each and every move to see what would happen. And it would keep exploring move after move for a while, forming a kind of HUGE decision tree of thousands of moves. And then it would come back along that tree, observing which moves seemed most likely to bring a good result.

But, what do we mean by "good result"? Well, Deep Blue had many carefully designed chess strategies built into it by expert chess players to help it make better decisions—for example, how to decide whether to protect the king or get advantage somewhere else? They made a specific "evaluation algorithm" for this purpose, to compare how advantageous or disadvantageous different board positions are (IBM hard-coded expert chess strategies into this evaluation function). Finally, it chose a carefully calculated move. On the next turn, it basically went through the whole thing again.

As you can see, this means Deep Blue thought about millions of theoretical positions before playing each move. This was not so impressive in terms of the AI software of Deep Blue, but rather in the hardware—IBM claimed it to be one of the most powerful computers available in the market at that time. It could look at 200 million board positions per second.

Now we come to Go. Just believe me that this game is much more open-ended, and if you tried the Deep Blue strategy on Go, you wouldn't be able to play well. There would be SO MANY positions to look at at each step that it would simply be impractical for a computer to go through that hell. For example, at the opening move in Chess, there are 20 possible moves. In Go, the first player has 361 possible moves, and this scope of choices stays wide throughout the game.

This means Go has an enormous "search space." Moreover, in Go, it's not so easy to judge how advantageous or disadvantageous a particular board position is at any specific point in the game—you kinda have to play the game for a long time before you can determine who has the upper hand. But let's say you magically had a way to do both of these. And that's where machine learning comes in!

So in this research, DeepMind used *neural networks* to do both of these tasks. Each neural network represents one *model,* which you learned about earlier. They trained a "policy neural network" to decide which are the most sensible moves in a particular board position (so it's like following an intuitive strategy to pick moves from any position). And they trained a "value neural network" to estimate how advantageous a particular board arrangement is for the player (in other words, how likely you are to win the game from this position). After defining what the models would *output,* they got to work figuring out what the inputs and internal architecture of the neural networks would be.

They trained these neural networks first with human game examples. After this the AI was able to mimic human playing to a certain degree, so it acted like a weak human player. Then to train the networks even further, they made the AI play against itself millions of times, trying to improve its score every time (called "reinforcement learning"). With this, the AI got better because it had more practice.

With these two networks alone, DeepMind's AI was able to play well against state-of-the-art Go playing programs that other researchers had built before. These other programs used an already popular pre-existing game-playing algorithm called "Monte Carlo Tree Search" (MCTS).

Playing Go in Japan, circa 1915. This is not an ordinary photo.

## Monte Carlo Tree Search (MCTS)

In this sub-section, we're getting a little into the weeds of AlphaGo. It's not that hard to understand (I'll try my best) and will improve your intuition, so stay with me! We're spending time here because I want you to get comfortable swimming in the deep end and not just walk away with surface-level understanding – that's what differentiates true innovators from armchair thought leaders.

Remember what I said about Deep Blue making a huge tree of millions of board positions and moves at each step of the game? It had to do simulations and look at and compare every possible move. As I said before, that was a simple and very straightforward approach—if the average software engineer had to design a game-playing program and had the most powerful computers in the world, she would probably design a similar solution.

But let's think about how humans themselves play chess? Let's say you're in the middle of the game at a particular board position. By game rules, you can do a dozen different things—move this pawn here, move the queen two squares here or three squares there, and so on. But do you really make a list of all the possible moves you can make with all your pieces, and then select one move from this long list? No—you "intuitively" narrow down to a few key moves (let's say you come up with three sensible moves) that you think make sense, and then you wonder what will happen in the game if you chose any of those three moves.

You might spend 15–20 seconds considering each of these moves and their future—and during these 15 seconds, you don't carefully plan out the future of each move; you can just "roll out" a few mental moves guided by your intuition without TOO much careful thought (well, a good player would think farther and more deeply than an average player). This is because you have limited time, *and* you can't accurately predict what your *opponent* will do at each step in that lovely future you're cooking up in your brain. So you'll just have to let your gut feeling guide you.

This part of your thinking process is called "rollout." After "rolling out" your few sensible moves, you finally say screw it and just play the move you find best.

Then the opponent makes a move. It might be a move you had already well anticipated, which means you are now pretty confident about what you need to do next. You don't have to spend too much time on the rollout again. OR, it could be that your opponent hits you with a pretty cool move that you had not expected, so you have to be even more careful with your next move.

This is how the game carries on, and as it gets closer and closer to the finishing point, it would get easier for you to predict the outcome of your moves—so your rollouts don't take as much time.

The purpose of this long story is to describe what the MCTS algorithm does on a superficial level—it mimics the above thinking process by building a "search tree" of moves and positions every time. The innovation here is that instead of going through all the possible moves at each position (which Deep Blue did), it instead intelligently selects a small set of sensible moves and explores those instead. To explore them, it "rolls out" the future of each of these moves and compares them based on their *imagined* outcomes.

Now let's come back to how this was used by AlphaGo.

Go is a "perfect information game" which means everyone can see what's happening on the board and nothing is hidden from either player, including the list of moves available to each player. *Theoretically,* for such games, no matter *which* particular position you are at in the game (even if you have just played 1–2 moves), it is possible that you can correctly guess who will win or lose assuming that both players play "perfectly" from that point on. (I have no idea who came up with this theory, but it was a fundamental assumption in this research project and it worked.)

That means, given a state of the game *s*, there is an "optimal value function" which can predict the outcome, let's say *probability* of you winning this game, from 0 to 1. Because some board positions are more likely to result in you winning than other board positions, they can be considered more "valuable" than the others. Let me say it again:

Value = Probability between 0 and 1 of you winning the game.

But wait—say there was a girl named Foma sitting next to you while you played Chess, and she kept telling you at each step if you were winning or losing. "You're winning... You're losing... Nope, still losing..." I think it wouldn't help you much in choosing which move you need to make. She would also be quite annoying. What would instead help you is if you drew the whole tree of all the possible moves you can make, and the states that those moves would lead to—and then Foma would tell you for the entire tree which states were winning states and which were losing states. Then you could choose moves which would keep leading you to winning states.

All of a sudden Foma becomes your partner in crime, not an annoying friend. Here, Foma behaves as your optimal value function. Earlier, it was believed that it's not possible to have an accurate value function like Foma for the game of Go, because the game had so much uncertainty. With AlphaGo, this assumption was proven false.

BUT—even if you had the wonderful Foma, this wonderland strategy of drawing out all the possible positions for Foma to evaluate will not work very well in the real world. In a game like Chess or Go, as we said before, if you try to imagine even 7–8 moves into the future, there can be so many possible positions to evaluate that you don't have enough time to check all of them with Foma.

So Foma is not enough. You need to narrow down the list of moves to a few sensible moves that you can roll out into the future. How will your program do that?

Enter Lusha. Lusha is a skilled Chess player and enthusiast who has spent decades watching grandmasters play Chess against each other. She can look at your board position, look quickly at all the available moves you can make, and tell you how likely it would be that a Chess *expert* would make any of those moves if they were sitting at your table. So if you have 50 possible moves at a given position, Lusha would tell you the probability that each would be picked by an expert.

Of course, a few sensible moves will have a high probability and other pointless moves will have very low probability. (For example: in Chess, let's say your Queen is in danger in one corner of the game. You might still have the option to move a little pawn in another corner, but it's unlikely that you would do so unless it directly helped save the queen or gained an advantage that outweighed her loss.)

So Lusha is your *policy function*. For a given state, she can give you probabilities for all the possible moves that an expert would make.

You can take Lusha's help to select a few sensible moves, and Foma will tell you the likelihood of winning from each of those moves! Using these two models can reduce the "search space" that Go is notorious for. These are the two most important "structural blocks" of this system.

These blocks could be implemented using any technology – recall from Chapter Eight how the technology you use for a given structural block can always evolve, as we saw with the payments example. By using deep neural networks to implement the policy and value functions, DeepMind accomplished a feat that changed human history.

DeepMind's AI used neural networks to make the MCTS algorithm work better. THIS improved variation of MCTS is "AlphaGo." Essentially, AlphaGo was simply an *improved implementation* of an ordinary algorithm designed by humans.

After some time, they introduced an even more powerful version called *AlphaGo Zero,* which beat AlphaGo in 100 consecutive games without losing a single one.

## Putting it all together

When building or designing AI systems, you have to manage an additional, parallel track of the development and training of AI models. This includes the following steps:

1.  Devise a sensible validation and verification strategy for your situation, and don't skip the initial work of systems engineering (as discussed in Chapters Four and Eight). Without that basis, you're not building a business, you're running a science project.

2.  Figure out why, how, and where machine learning is a good tool for the problem you're trying to solve – while there is no formula for this, you can usually use the yardstick of "would it be easier to show than to tell?" Having a good sense of functional and structural blocks will greatly help with this step. Usually, it's good to start by defining the OUTPUTS you need, and then figuring out what models and inputs you need to produce them.

3.  Choose the right models to train: this requires you to do open-ended research, make assumptions and test them, or build on top of models that others have already developed. This is the most "science-y" part of building AI systems. Most AI projects involve a little R&D by default.

4.  Set up the pipeline of data that will be used to train the models, or to build a simulator environment where the models can train themselves with artificial examples. This also extends to having the right databases and information management systems in place. THIS is the most important part of building AI systems. Without the right examples, the models can't be trained properly, so you should spend probably 80 percent of your time and energy on this step.

5.  Create a feedback loop, so that the system keeps improving over time as you find new data (from clients or elsewhere) and develop better models.

Depending on the novelty, ambition, and size of the undertaking, these steps can get quite expensive, because you also need dedicated infrastructure for large AI experiments – a project like AlphaGo can run into millions of dollars, without even counting the salaries of world-class scientists and engineers.

## "Digital Transformation"

Now here's a very interesting bit. The above steps work really well when you're building an AI system from scratch, for a new product. But what if you already have an established company doing its thing, and want to introduce AI to benefit various parts of your business? What if your goal is to *digitally transform* an existing business in incremental ways, instead of doing something disruptive?

Somewhat counter-intuitively, for that, you'd have to follow the above steps *in reverse*.

First, make sure you're gathering as much data from your various business processes as possible. Without data, there is no AI project. Here's what that means practically:

- If you deal with paper documents, start digitizing them. There are various AI vendors on the market to help you smartly digitize everything from receipts and invoices to X-ray scans of metal parts from your manufacturing line. (I know the CEOs of many of these companies through the Age of AI Podcast, so you can check it out.)

- Have a sensible database strategy and consider investing in other forms of storage (such as "data warehouses" and "data lakes") to make sure all your business activity data is query-able and usable. When your company has a habit of generating and storing data and treating it like a first-order citizen, it's much easier to develop new AI and other digital systems on top.

With a data strategy and infrastructure in place, you can start looking at the different functional and structural blocks of your business, and identify areas of improvement or new strategic ideas.

Now you can hire data scientists or ML engineers to create models that are not only inline with your business priorities, but are also easier to build because much of the data infrastructure they'd need would be readily available. It also becomes easier to shop around for new AI solutions being built by innovative startups. (Just like you need a certain level of plumbing in your house to be able to install a modern toilet, many startups can only sell you their products if you have a minimum level of digitization already!)

I should also mention here that I do NOT recommend you create a "data science team" or "machine learning team" in your company. Instead of putting all the ML folks in one separate team, place each of them right within the business unit or product team that they're going to be working with. Your ML engineers should be seen as contributors to a product team, and have the same goals and be held to the same deadlines as the other team members, not working on a separate thread doing science projects. This way, their efforts will be focused on real problems that other people in the company actually care about. You're building a business, not a research lab like DeepMind or OpenAI.

As the AI experiments begin to show promise, you can mature as a digital organization and do bigger things with technology. As you start to become a serious AI organization, then just like DevOps (tooling and processes you invest in to help devs ship better code faster and more reliably), you'll probably want to invest in "MLOps," which involves putting systems in place so that your ML engineers and data scientists can easily build, train, and ship high-quality models. (I think the day is not far when we come full circle and create *OpsOps* – operations people who help you handle all the *other* operations people you've stuffed your company with.)

———◆———

While I can't possibly do justice to the entire field of AI in a single chapter, I hope it was at least able to nudge and inspire you to take it seriously as a powerful, strategic tool that can support all your future endeavors.

I think that the rise of Artificial Intelligence is not only a tool for business but the next big step in our evolution as a species altogether. It changes everything we thought was possible. But I also believe that the "secret sauce" of AI is human creativity, imagination, and endeavor. Well, at least for the time being.

Artist: Pablo Martínez (Venezuela)

*Scan this artwork like a QR code for optional bonus content.*

# RECAP

Are you feeling overwhelmed? As promised in the beginning of the book, we've covered a lot of ground already. So let's do a quick review.

Your journey of technical fluency really began in Chapter One itself, where you saw that all technical decisions should ultimately be grounded in the business strategy. Without the latter, the former turns into nothing more than a science project. Business is, at its core, about trading something of value, so it helps to not lose sight of that fundamental reality.

Chapter Two was an introduction to the book and its premise.

In Chapter Three, you got a very broad overview of the entire field of software engineering. You learned about how computers work, what software and "code" really is, a little about programming languages, and stacks, the internet being a "highway," and the global economy of software (with frameworks and APIs for most things so you don't have to reinvent the wheel). You also looked at some basic factors that influence software design.

In Chapter Four, we shifted gears a bit to discuss the human aspects of real-world software engineering. We saw engineering and entrepreneurship through a new lens, that of risk management. We also studied project management from first-principles, without being biased towards any popular methodology. Through case studies of the FBI's VCF and Sentinel projects, you got a sense of what can go wrong and what to watch out for. The three key concepts we covered were how to choose a sensible validation strategy, the importance of technical architecture, and the hidden force of "engineering culture."

In Chapter Five, we came back to technical topics, first through a deep dive into databases and "information management." You learned about database schemas, how they affect the business directly, the challenges of scaling data storage, and some new paradigms such as NoSQL.

In Chapter Six, we took things up a notch, talking about *scale*. You saw how scaling anything, whether you're selling cocaine cocktails or growing a dating website, is not an exact science, but shares the same fundamentals and trade-offs. You learned about splitting the load, caching, content delivery networks and other concepts and technologies.

Chapter Seven took you to the world of cyber crime. You learned to see attacks and defence from a whole new perspective, and got a taste of what it's like to think like a mischief-maker. You looked at the anatomy of the Target hack and saw how it was like a sophisticated bank heist. We also went over some common types of attacks and strategies to defend against them.

Chapter Eight was about smartly using system design to yield tremendous competitive advantages, as well as help tech projects succeed better. We stepped out from the technical depth and had a long discussion about systems engineering, architecture, and many practical "how-to" aspects of building tech. You got some indirect practice using tools like context diagrams, functional flow, non-functional requirements, structural blocks and services. We also had a brief discussion around choosing the right software stack or programming languages, and its business implications.

Chapter Nine introduced you to more of the day-to-day activities involved in running and managing a productive dev team. You learned about methods and processes such as version control, testing and deployment strategy, code refactoring, and documentation, and got the essence of DevOps.

Lastly, Chapter Ten was about AI. You learned about the concept of "models," which is central to machine learning, how models are trained, and how to use them in creative ways to solve problems (using the detailed AlphaGo case study). You also got a flexible, broadly applicable plan for how to actually go about doing new AI projects, and how to prepare your company for an AI-powered future.

Moreover, in additional "interludes" throughout the book, you learned how the internet works, how to gain healthy influence over experts through a simple four-word phrase, and a fascinating framework (albeit rooted in violent animal experiments) to help you make product roadmapping decisions.

Now, time to wrap up!

———◆———

# The Beginning

In Japan, the home of most popular martial arts, a black belt has an interesting significance. While people in other countries see it as a towering achievement that demonstrates mastery and commands a certain level of respect, in Japan, it's seen as only the *beginning* of your real martial arts journey. It simply means you have a good command of the basics and can now chart your own path towards true mastery as you continue to learn from others and develop your unique style.

With that, I heartily congratulate you on getting to the end of this book!

You've earned a sort of black belt in your own right. While this book may have only taken you a few days to finish, it shortcuts many months, if not *years* of learning done the conventional way, so you're allowed to feel more "dangerous" than before you began this journey! In fact, when it comes to making strategic, business-critical technology decisions, you're probably better equipped at this point than most junior software engineers (who have spent a lot of time developing the skills of programming but not enough time learning how to use technology) and even many senior product managers.

From today onwards, if someone asks if you're "technical," you can confidently respond without missing a beat, *"yes I'm tech fluent; what about it?"*

And yet, I encourage you to see this as just the beginning of your journey. Use this knowledge as a good conceptual base, and continue to build on it. Read this book again after a few weeks to deepen your understanding of the concepts.

To help you on the rest of your journey, here's some more advice:

- Most of our acquisition of technical knowledge comes from reading technical articles and documents and trying to make sense of them. It's not always easy, and even the best engineers and scientists struggle at times. But often, technical content can seem intimidating at first glance. The key to getting over this is to *read at different levels of abstraction*:

  Start by skimming over the jargon and just trying to understand what the overall context is, and what the article's goal is. If it's trying to teach you how to use a tool to get a particular result, what is that result? If it's comparing an old technique with a new approach, what's the purpose of using either method and the basis of comparison? Once you have this high-level context, when you have a good grasp of why that article was written, you can try to study in-depth what it's really saying.

- *Keep your humility in check*. Give yourself permission to act confidently in meetings. If you're feeling lost during a technical discussion, it's not a cue to fall silent, zone out and curl up in a ball; it's a cue for you to interrupt the conversation and ask them to help you hop back on the train wherever you got left out. You can use the same technique as mentioned above: First, make sure you understand the context and what the discussion is trying to achieve. What's the goal, and what's at stake? Recenter the conversation around that and ask them to fill in the rest of the gaps.

- Software engineering can feel highly subjective at times, much like any other branch of science or technology. Developers often disagree with each other and are inconsistent about how things should be done, what they consider good or bad, etc. Embrace this! It means that you can and probably should negotiate with them when they say something that doesn't make sense to you (i.e. try to understand WHY they hold a certain technical opinion). Often when engineers tell you that something "can't be done," they're really saying, "I don't know how to do it." How you handle these situations depends on your leadership style.

- You should assume the job of teaching new non-technical executives in your company about how your technology works overall, before they get an in-depth orientation from the engineers. It will keep you sharp. Just consider it. You won't be doing it forever, just a few times.

- Don't let the technical wizardry obscure the essential: *being a student of your trade.* Technology ultimately exists to help you offer a better deal to your important trading partners. Tech serves the business, not the other way around.

When I write, I always imagine that you, my reader, are sitting across from me and we're having a conversation. It's the weirdest thing ever, but as you finish reading this book, I feel a little bittersweet, like ending a long delightful chat with an old friend.

I wish I had some "inspiring" words for you, but this is all I have for now:

Building a business and chasing your ambitions can be hard. Regardless of which stage you are at right now, I want you to know that I am with you on your journey. I extend to you a warm hand of friendship across the vast space and time that may separate us, and wish that something great happens to you today that makes you smile.

——◆——

# *In Remembrance*

My mother was more of an entrepreneur, educator, engineer, artist, and polymath than I can ever hope to be.

She got a dual Masters degree in mathematics and computer science, and opened a "computing skills" institute in New Delhi, India long before it was cool. At a time when most people we knew had never used or even seen a computer, we had eight PCs in our little home office. It was a dream business — the right solution, the right person, and the right time. Despite being bootstrapped and profitable from day one, the business grew so quickly that my parents often had to turn away large customers.

And then one day, my mother abruptly stopped. She shut down the company. She wanted to spend more time with me and my sister, who were both very little at the time. She sacrificed her future for ours.

I realized only recently that much of what I do today, including this book, is simply a faint shadow of what she was doing decades ago. I didn't realize it until I was working mid-way through the book. It is her legacy more than mine.

I inherited from her the heart of a teacher, her passion for introducing others to the wonders of technology, her extraordinary variety of interests and knowledge, and her willingness to make new friends everywhere she went. (Unfortunately, I didn't inherit her talent for mathematics. But then my sister didn't either, so at least it doesn't sting. #SiblingRivalry)

If you enjoyed learning from me, you now know who deserves all the credit. Thank you for reading.

# Acknowledgements

Let me ask you a question. How often do you take stock of all the people you are thankful to – people who helped you unconditionally at some point in your life?

This book, just like everything else I've ever accomplished, was only possible because of the overwhelming kindness and generosity of others.

For me, writing this "acknowledgments" page was a unique, intensely emotional experience. I've never thanked so many people all at once! I learned how powerful gratitude can be.

I encourage you to write your own acknowledgments page sometime, even if you never intend to publish it anywhere.

First and foremost: my father and sister. Thank you for everything.

Then, my "partners in crime" who pushed me to finish this book and have been an anchor of support behind this project: John Lester, Brett Oliver, Ziyuan "Isabella" Wang, Amit Tripathi, Nick Kaeshko, and Otar Berejiani. Your faith gave me strength. Thank you!

My dearest colleagues, present and former, some of whom even volunteered to work for free during times when business was tough: Bami Osidele, Liza Mankovskaya, Armine Papikyan, Harry Bishop, Nané Avedikian, Jenny Olarte... Thank you. I'm proud of you all.

This book was an extremely unusual cross-cultural creative endeavour. For this I thank my talented designers and artists from around the planet, who with their skills and selfless devotion turned it into a thing of beauty I can proudly show to the entire world: Marisha Vadera (India), Iram Ahmed (Pakistan), Anne-Sophie Balestrini (France), Ammie Govers (USA), Janet Freysoldt (Canada), Inan Anjum Sibun (Bangladesh), Alena Lundberg (USA), Raquel Paolini Madrid (Venezuela), Gihantha Gunasekara (Sri Lanka), Ryn Ortega (USA), Pablo Martínez (Venezuela), M. Lutfi' As'ad, S.Si. (Indonesia), and Sophie Pakeliani (Georgia). This list doesn't even mention 20+ more designers — again distributed across 6 continents — whose direct inputs indirectly shaped this book.

The men who took chances on me early on, when I was switching careers every few months: Vardhan Koshal, Randy Rayess, Pratham Mittal, Sampath Mallidi, Josh Winnegrad, Balaji Vishwanathan, Ashwin Kumar, Kevin Keogh, Walter Stockman, and Jon Wilfong to name a few. Thank you.

My good friends and support network, who were always there to encourage me: Anirudh Bhaikhel, Siddharth Sharma, Mike Doubintchik, Dikshant Chitkara, Ujjwal Varadarajan, Wilson Llivichuzhca, Arghya Malya Roy, Suranjan Jena, Vaibhav Chhipa, Lina Zhu, James Ingallinera, Irene Alvarado, Linda Brandt, Robert Oda, and Weilu Xu. Your words meant more than you realize. Thank you.

All the people I've had the fortune to teach and have as clients – I can't name you, but you know who you are. Thank you for giving me a chance to serve.

The teachers who invested in me: Dr. Niteesh Sahni, Dr. N. Sukumar, Dr. Amit Ray, Dr. Nishant Mishra, Stephen and Jane Kelly, Doug Green, Bruce Cota, Xu Li, Ashwin Ramanathan, Dr. Kirstin Petersen, Dr. Dave Schneider, Robert Newman, Brad Treat, Sangeeta Negi... Thank you for having the heart of a teacher.

Then, the countless people whose inputs made this book's content and message better (it's mind-blowing how many people have touched this book in some way):

Wilson Mvula, Connie Chu, Taylor Kennon, Sarah Proctor, Jacob Carter, Alice Tsai, Dhruv Baldawa, Alicia Butler Pierre, Robert Oda, Marisa Huston,

Taly Matiteyahu, Robert Lakeberg, Keith Melkild, Andrew Latimer, Justin Bouldin, Kathryn Engelhardt-Cronk, Katelin Cherry, David Pereira, Albert Swantner, Chris Miller, Tatiana Fofanova, Dan Brigham, Gerard Butler, Lydia Sugarman, Kayode Abass, Jennifer Tkachuk-Tremblay Stasiewich, Peyman Shahmirzadi, Don Hammond, Tony Zirnoon, Uwe Kannemacher, Kevin Jacobs, Mayukh Nair, Alexandra Stolzenberger, Aytaç Bildik, Gohar Ohanyan, Roberta Certini, Ann Li, Meredith, Chiachee Lee, Jarie Bolander, Natsune Otsuki, Johanna Pagonis, Dave Monk, Garrett and Ceata Lash, Steve Sponseller, Craig Staley, Andrew Miller, Taylor Marks, Hannah Lockwood, Dustin Miller, Michelle Nedelec, Roseann Galvan, Mark Stinson, Mike Steward, Zack Hudson, Bianca Wulwick, Sharon Jones, Bonnie Graham, Steve Pappas, Christina Nitschmann-Rivera, Wanda Wallace, Folu Owolabi, Tosin Leye, Toyin Olasehinde, Stephen Nwachukwu, Jude Akhabue, Ikechi Odigbo, Darcy DeClute, Rose Davidson... Thank you!

The countless generous professionals whose advice and resources educated and supported me through this book's writing, editing, and publication processes: there are too many to name here, but special mention goes to the talented teams at Scribe Media, Reedsy, IngramSpark, and 99Designs.

Lastly, I thank two authors whose passionate writing and teaching styles influenced me as a kid in school, and helped me make better friends with my inner nerd: Jearl Walker and Kjartan Poskitt. You are the OGs. Thank you.

I wonder if there are any truly "self-made" people in this world. But I know one thing for sure: I am not one of them.

# About the Author

Aman Y. Agarwal is the Founder and President of SANPRAM Transnational, an umbrella corporation driving various projects in technology, education, research, and media. He's also the host of The Eccentric CEO and The Age of AI Podcasts.

You can find him on: aman-agarwal.com

Printed in Great Britain
by Amazon

11343896R00114